Cross Stitch & Needlepoint Chart and Pattern Sketchbook

× × ×

Four Sizes of Stitch Count Graphs
On 10 Square Grid
With Fill In Floss Charts

Hoop & Thread Needlework Design

Copyright © 2019 Hoop & Thread Needlework Design
Arisa Williams and Kim O'Malley
All rights reserved.
ISBN: 9781795621861

CONTENTS

1   100 x 120 Stitch Count 10-Square Graph Grids   Pg 1

2   80 x 100 Stitch Count 10-Square Graph Grids   Pg 43

3   60 x 80 Stitch Count 10-Square Graph Grids   Pg 85

4   40 x 60 Stitch Count 10-Square Graph Grids   Pg 127

100 X 120 Stitch Count

10-Square Graph Grids

Floss Chart

	STRAND	TYPE	NUMBER	COLOR	ALTERNATE
•					
○					
■					
✚					
△					
◆					
=					
✖					
★					
⊙					
◘					
#					
▼					
▢					
▢					
▽					
→					
☽					

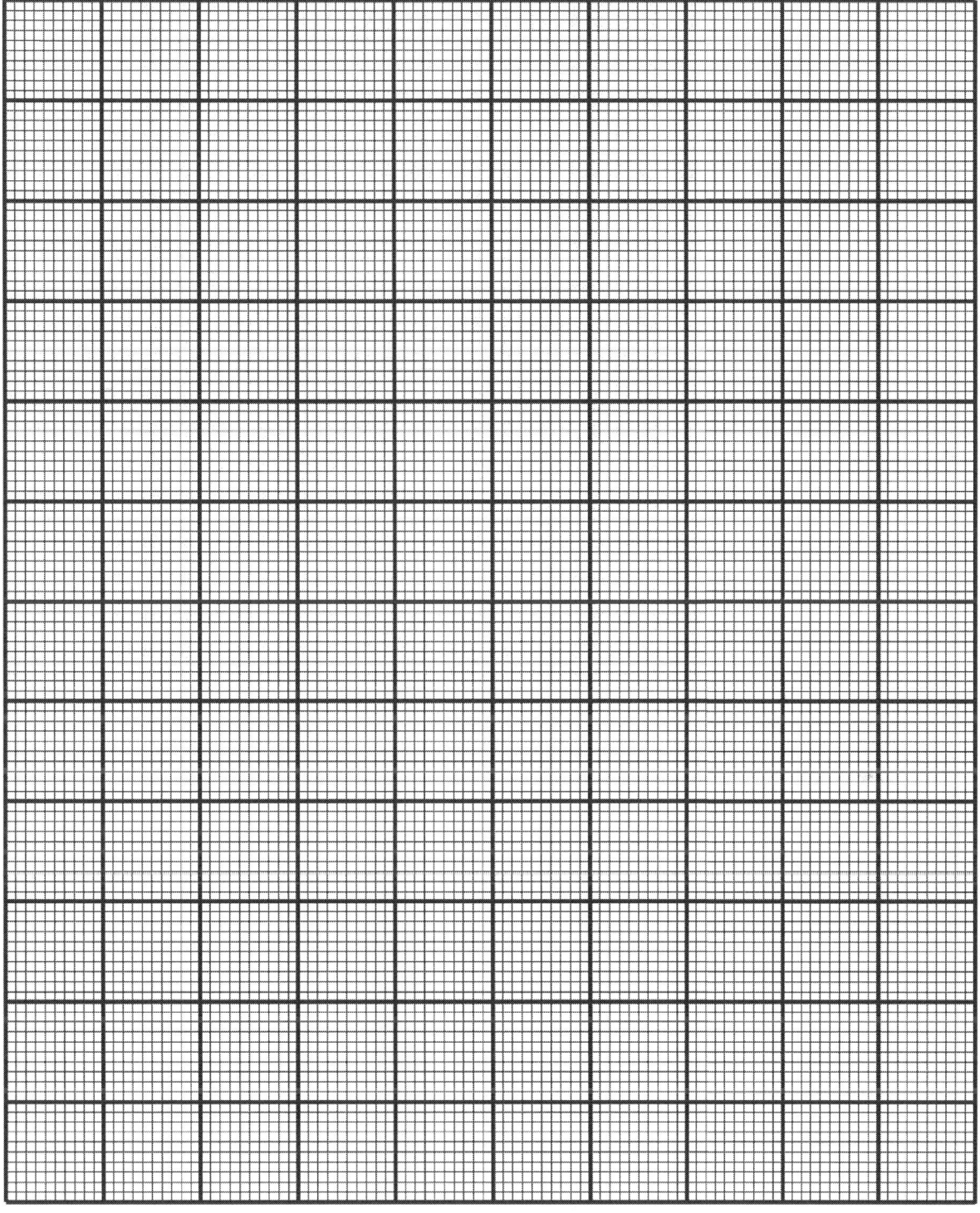

Floss Chart

	STRAND	TYPE	NUMBER	COLOR	ALTERNATE
•					
○					
■					
✚					
△					
◆					
=					
✖					
★					
⊙					
▫					
#					
▼					
☐					
☐					
▽					
→					
☾					

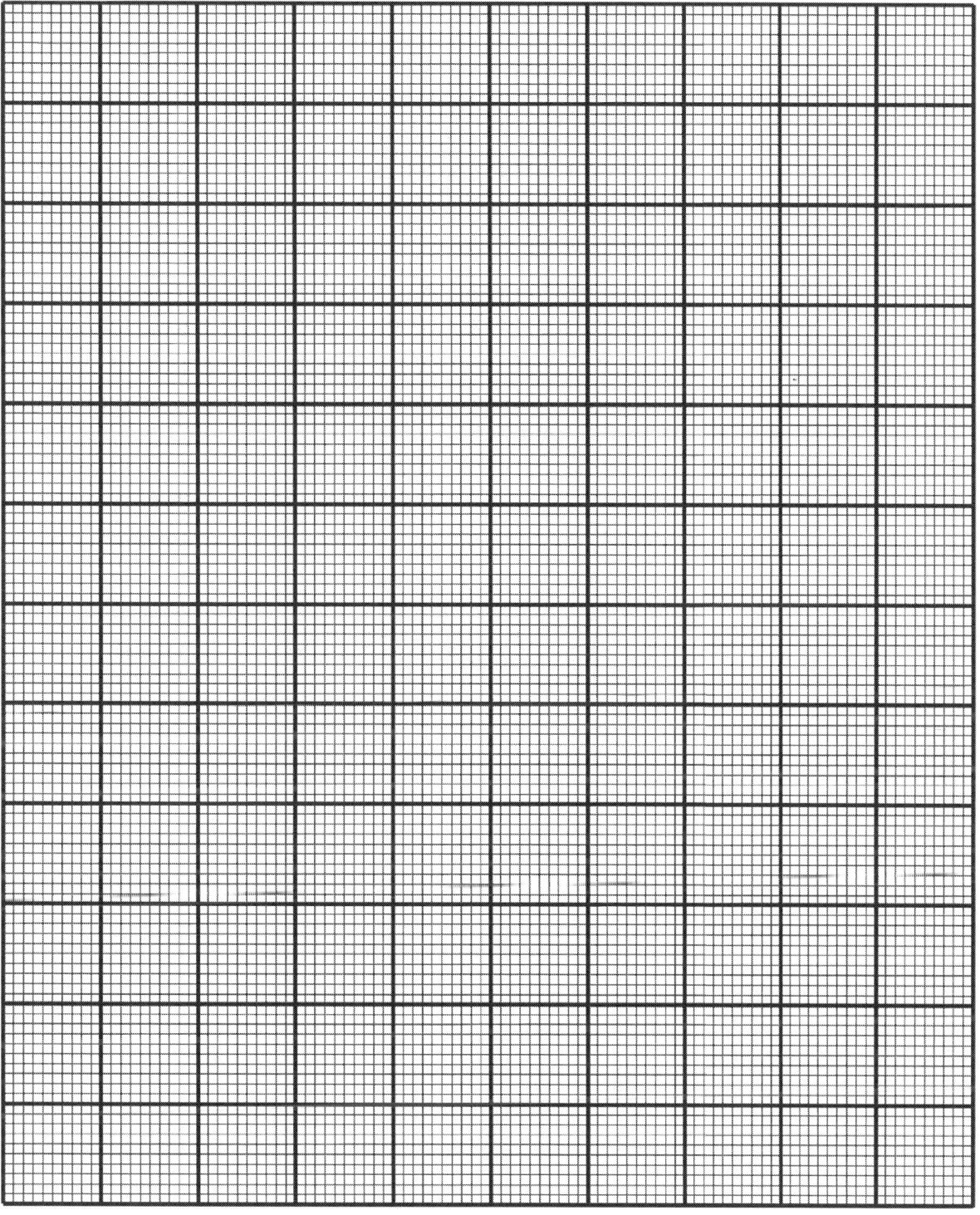

Floss Chart

	STRAND	TYPE	NUMBER	COLOR	ALTERNATE
•					
○					
■					
✚					
△					
◆					
=					
✖					
★					
⊙					
▫					
#					
▼					
□					
□					
▽					
→					
☽					

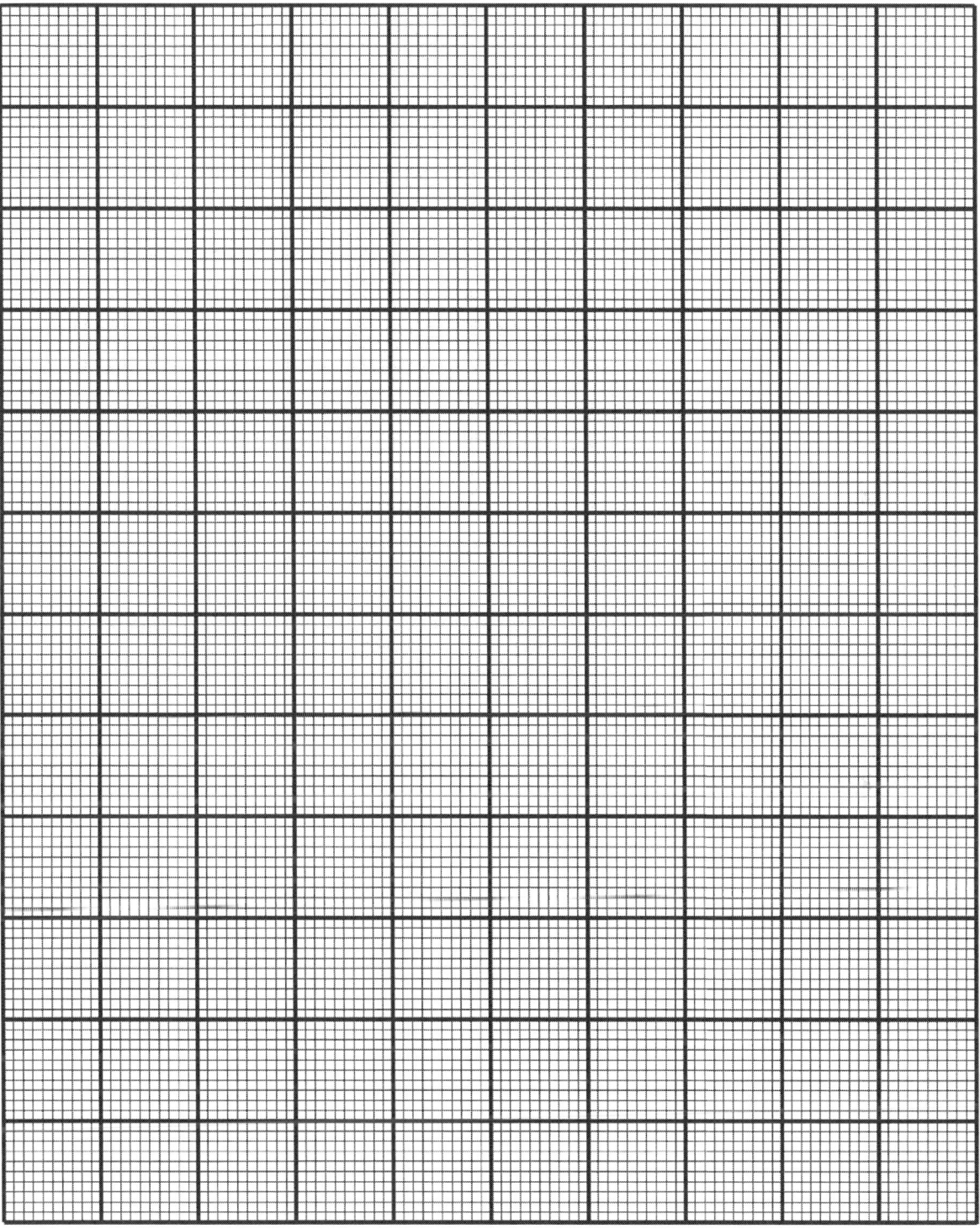

Floss Chart

	STRAND	TYPE	NUMBER	COLOR	ALTERNATE
•					
○					
■					
✚					
△					
◆					
=					
✖					
★					
⊙					
▣					
#					
▼					
▫					
▫					
▽					
→					
☽					

Floss Chart

	STRAND	TYPE	NUMBER	COLOR	ALTERNATE
•					
○					
■					
✛					
△					
◆					
=					
✖					
★					
⊙					
▫					
#					
▼					
☐					
☐					
▽					
→					
☽					

CROSS STITCH & NEEDLEPOINT CHART AND PATTERN SKETCHBOOK

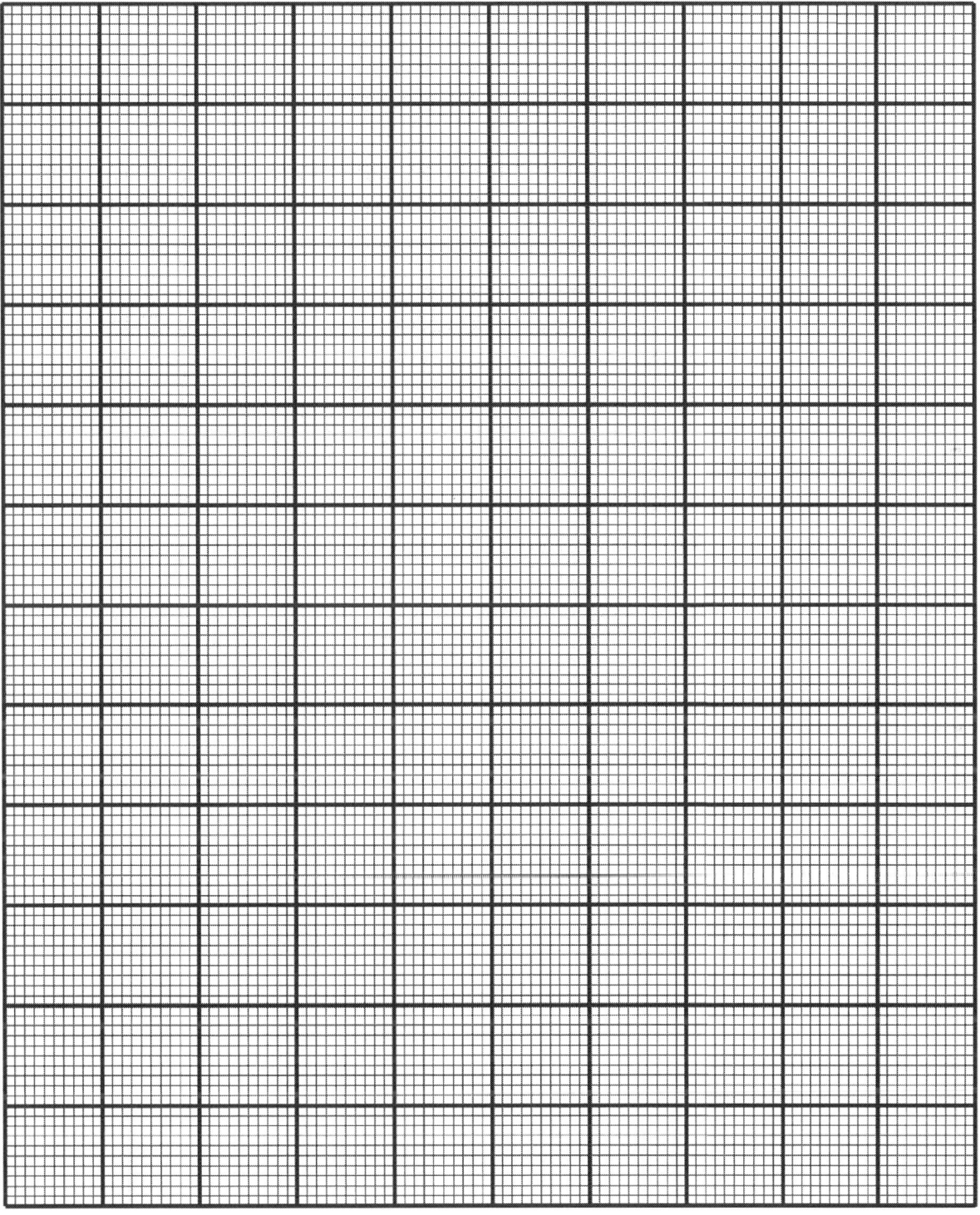

Floss Chart

	STRAND	TYPE	NUMBER	COLOR	ALTERNATE
•					
○					
■					
✚					
△					
◆					
=					
✖					
★					
⊙					
⊟					
#					
▼					
☐					
☐					
▽					
→					
☽					

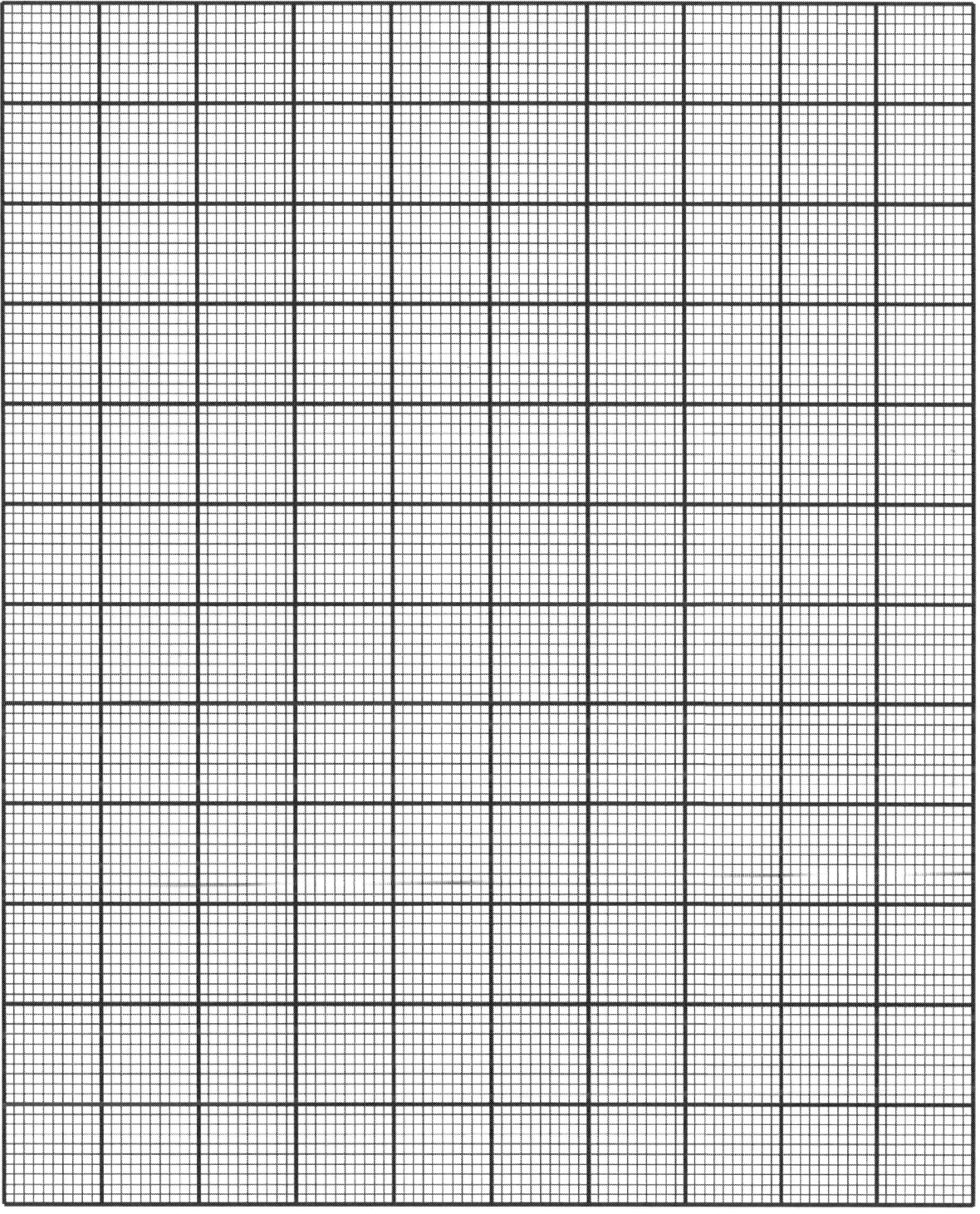

Floss Chart

	STRAND	TYPE	NUMBER	COLOR	ALTERNATE
•					
○					
■					
✚					
△					
◆					
=					
✖					
★					
⊙					
❒					
#					
▼					
☐					
☐					
▽					
→					
☾					

Floss Chart

	STRAND	TYPE	NUMBER	COLOR	ALTERNATE
•					
○					
■					
✚					
△					
◆					
=					
✖					
★					
⊙					
▣					
#					
▼					
□					
□					
▽					
→					
☽					

Floss Chart

	STRAND	TYPE	NUMBER	COLOR	ALTERNATE
•					
○					
■					
✚					
△					
◆					
=					
✖					
★					
⊙					
◘					
#					
▼					
☐					
☐					
▽					
→					
☽					

Floss Chart

	STRAND	TYPE	NUMBER	COLOR	ALTERNATE
•					
○					
■					
✚					
△					
◆					
=					
✖					
★					
⊙					
▣					
#					
▼					
□					
□					
▽					
→					
☽					

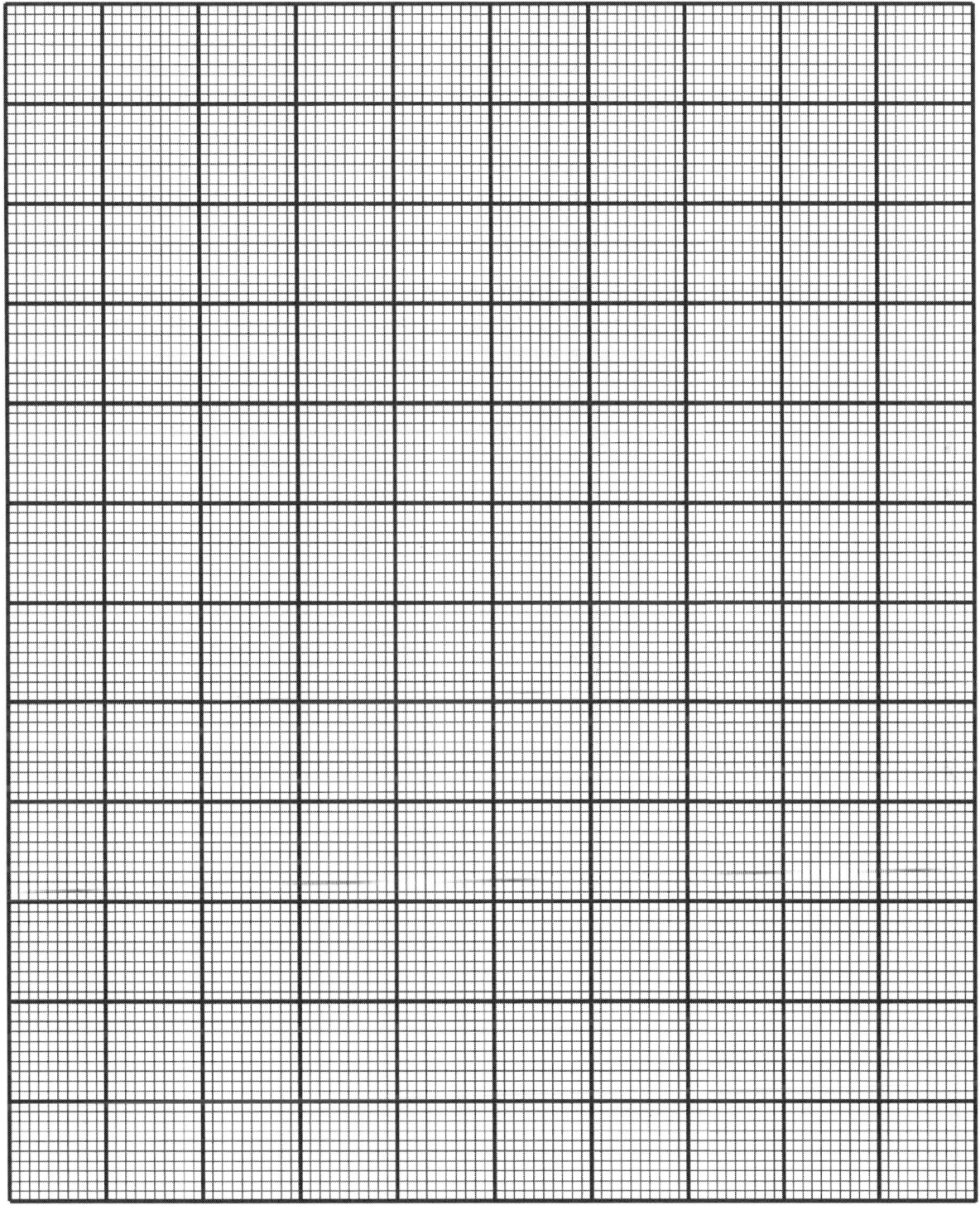

Floss Chart

	STRAND	TYPE	NUMBER	COLOR	ALTERNATE
•					
○					
■					
✚					
△					
◆					
=					
✖					
★					
⊙					
▫					
#					
▼					
□					
□					
▽					
→					
☽					

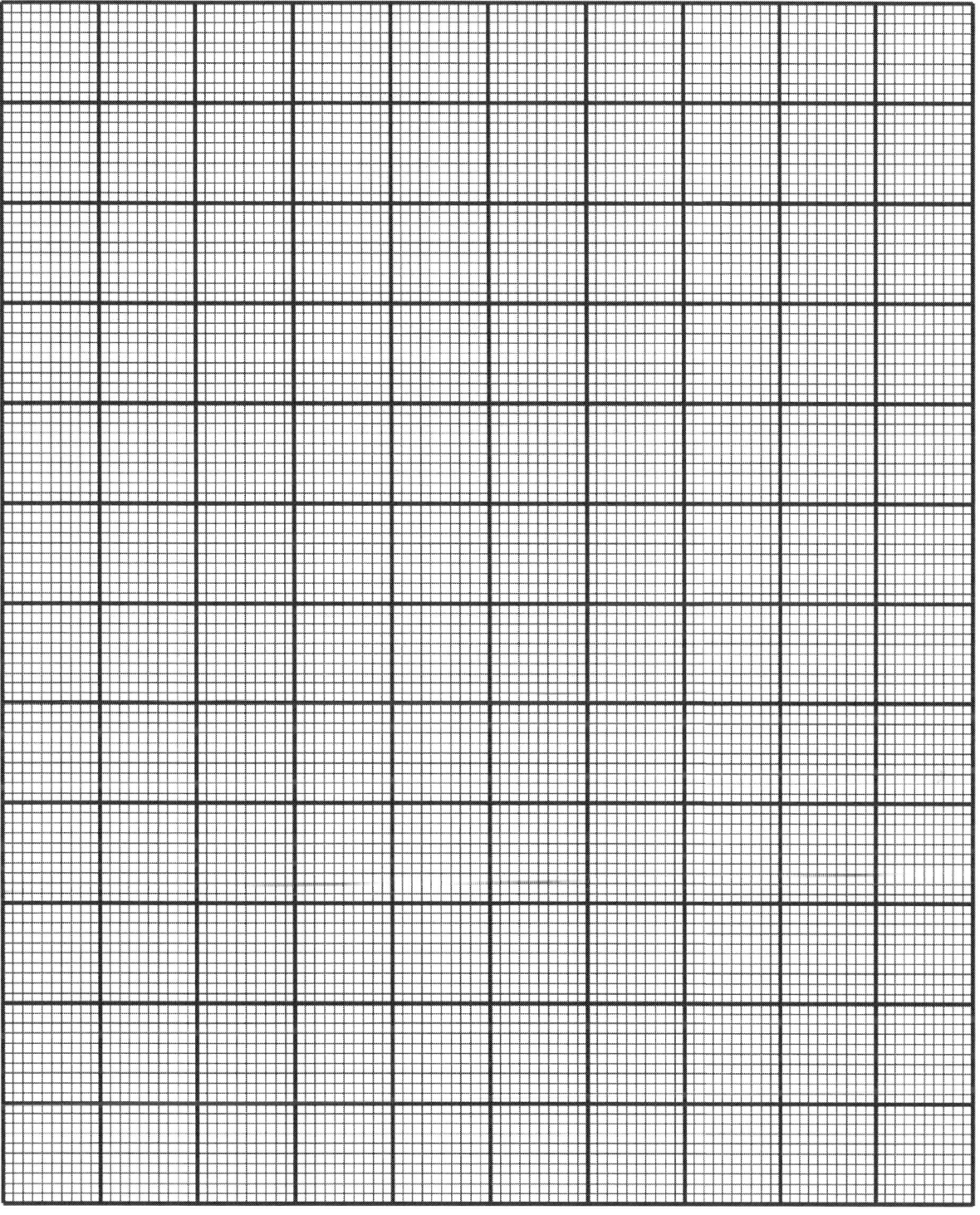

Floss Chart

	STRAND	TYPE	NUMBER	COLOR	ALTERNATE
•					
○					
■					
✚					
△					
◆					
=					
✖					
★					
⊙					
▣					
#					
▼					
□					
□					
▽					
→					
☽					

Floss Chart

	STRAND	TYPE	NUMBER	COLOR	ALTERNATE
•					
○					
■					
✚					
△					
◆					
=					
✖					
★					
⊙					
▫					
#					
▼					
☐					
☐					
▽					
→					
☽					

Floss Chart

	STRAND	TYPE	NUMBER	COLOR	ALTERNATE
•					
○					
■					
✚					
△					
◆					
=					
✖					
★					
⊙					
▣					
#					
▼					
□					
□					
▽					
→					
☽					

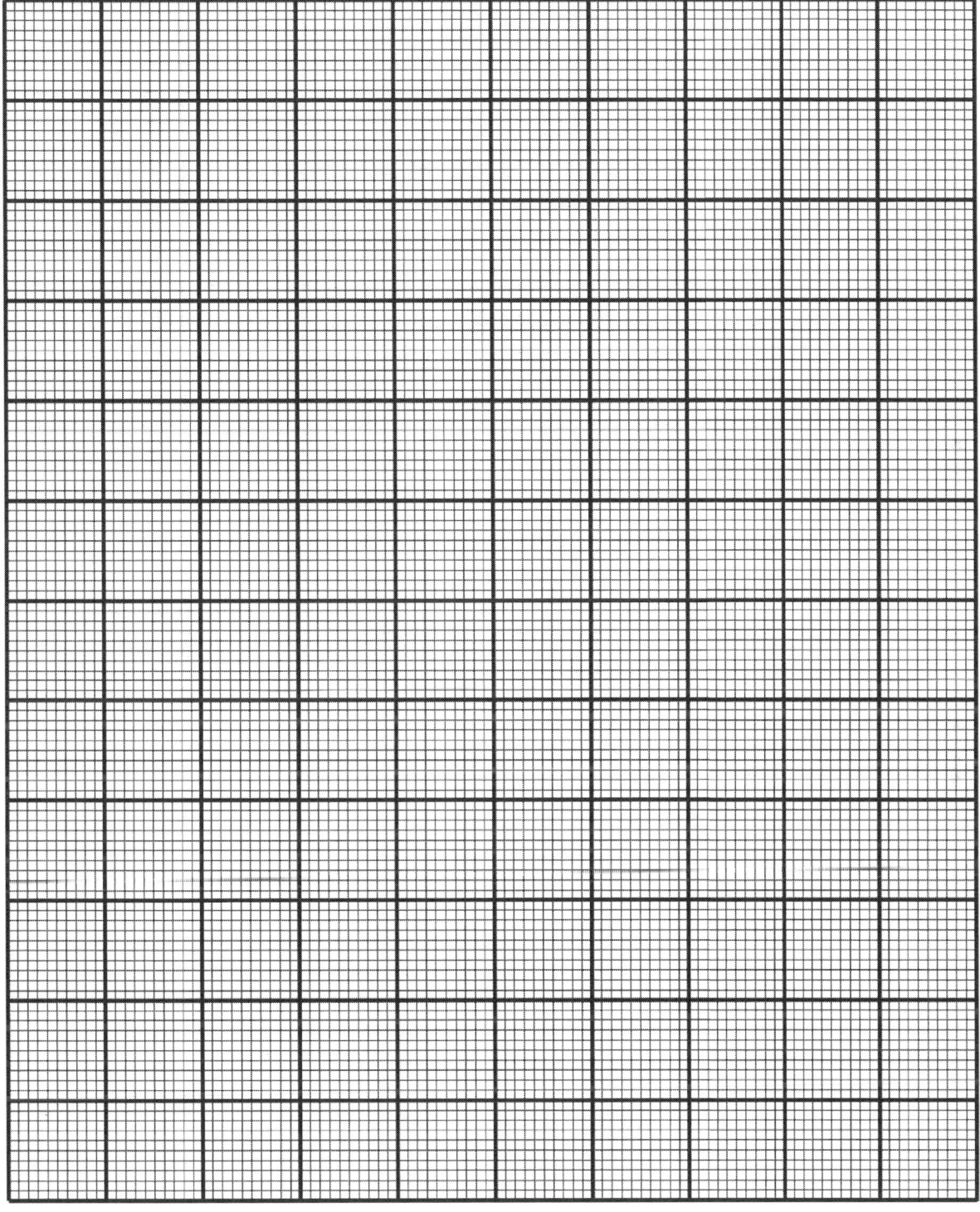

Floss Chart

	STRAND	TYPE	NUMBER	COLOR	ALTERNATE
•					
○					
■					
✚					
△					
◆					
=					
✖					
★					
⊙					
▣					
#					
▼					
□					
□					
▽					
→					
☾					

Floss Chart

	STRAND	TYPE	NUMBER	COLOR	ALTERNATE
•					
○					
■					
✚					
△					
◆					
=					
✖					
★					
⊙					
◲					
#					
▼					
☐					
☐					
▽					
→					
☾					

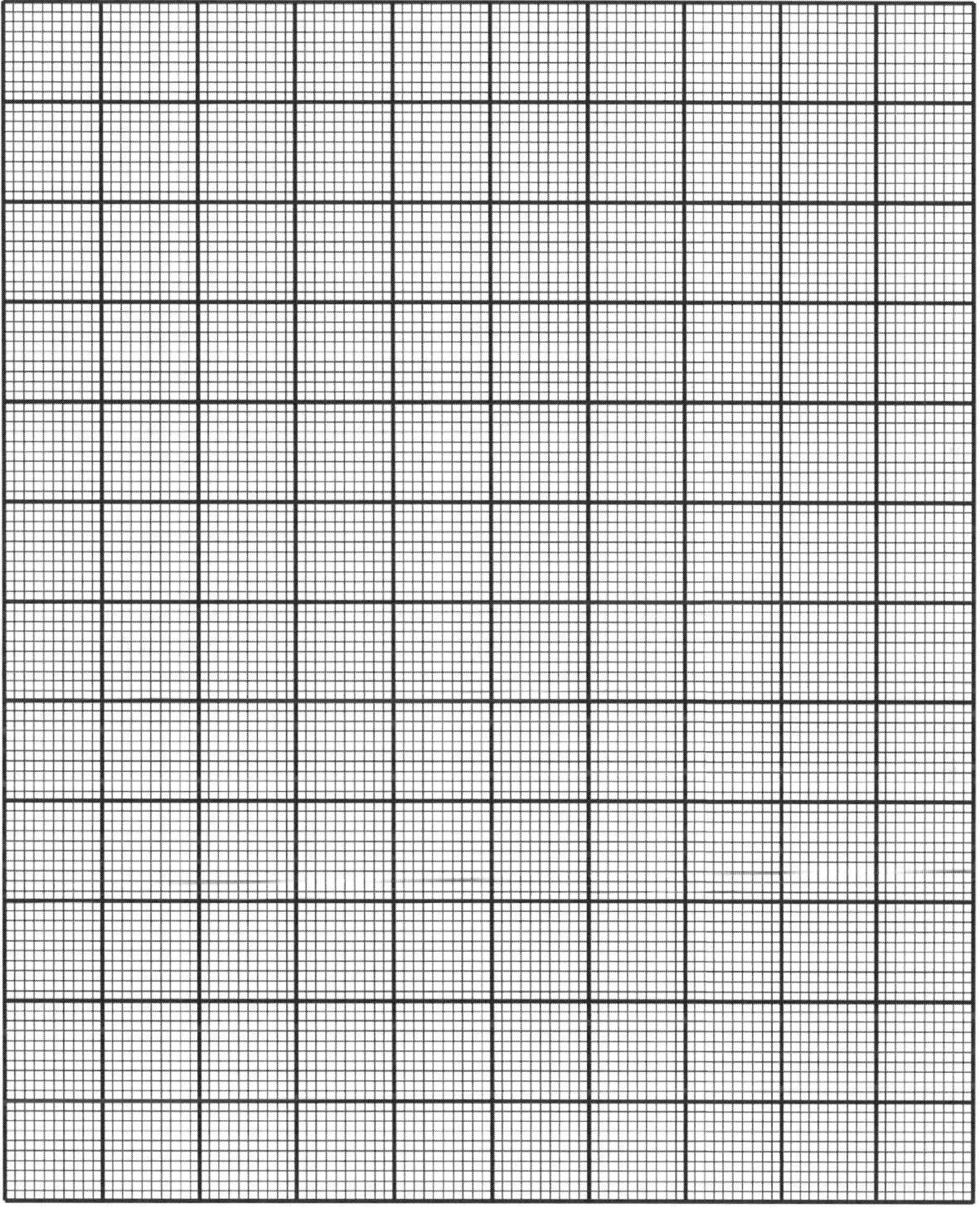

Floss Chart

	STRAND	TYPE	NUMBER	COLOR	ALTERNATE
•					
○					
■					
✚					
△					
◆					
=					
✖					
★					
⊙					
▣					
#					
▼					
□					
□					
▽					
→					
☽					

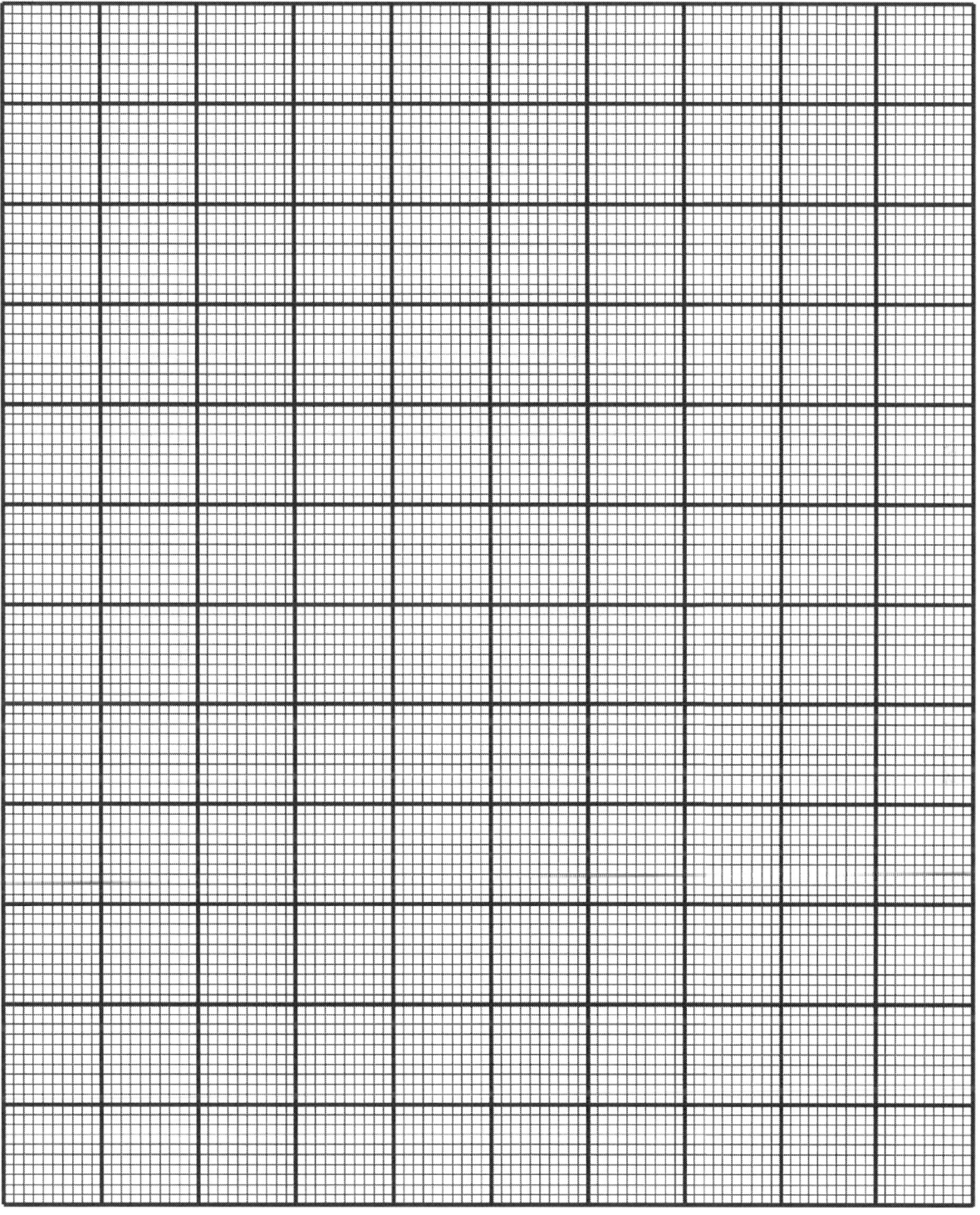

Floss Chart

	STRAND	TYPE	NUMBER	COLOR	ALTERNATE
•					
○					
■					
✚					
△					
◆					
=					
✖					
★					
⊙					
▣					
#					
▼					
☐					
☐					
▽					
→					
☽					

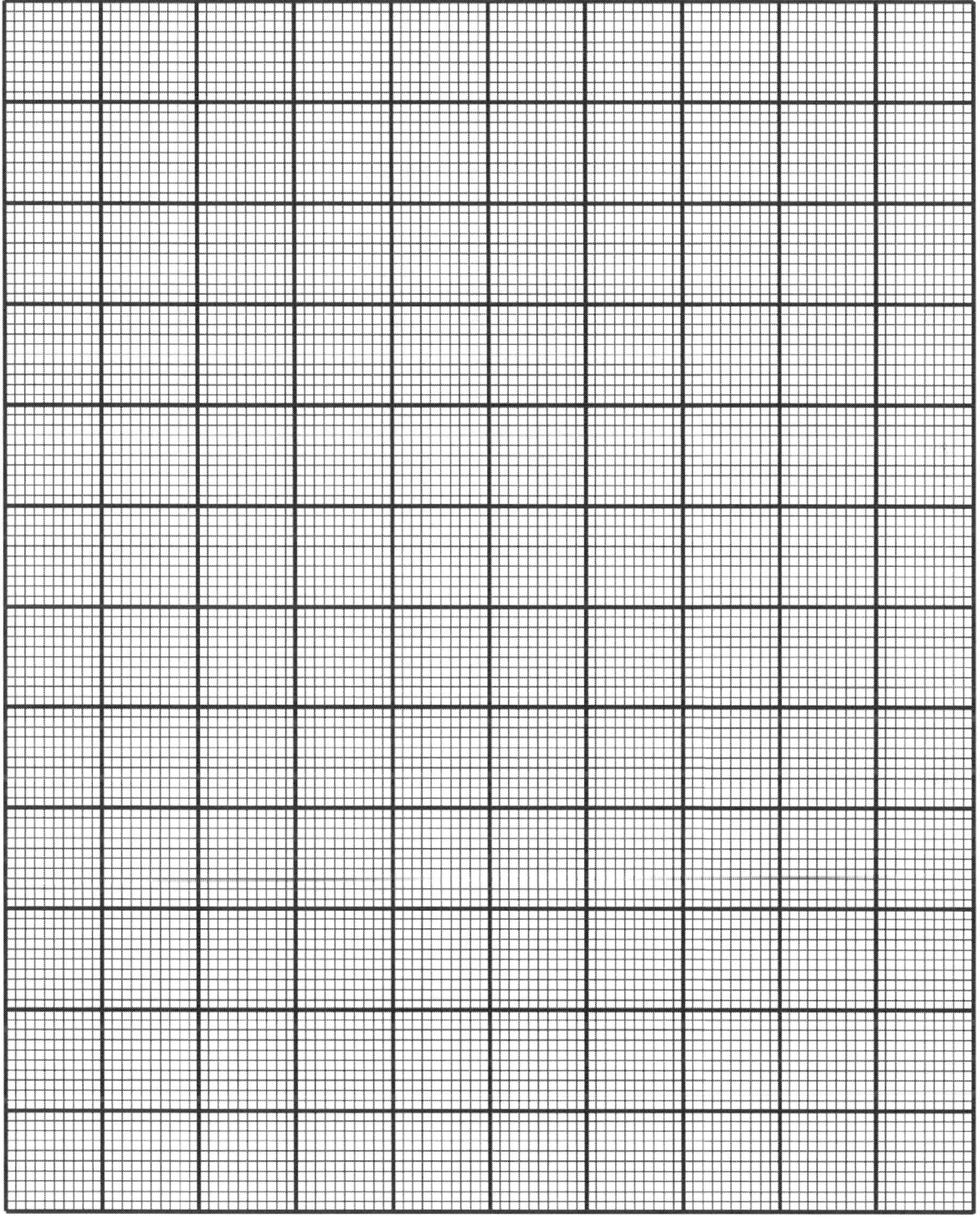

Floss Chart

	STRAND	TYPE	NUMBER	COLOR	ALTERNATE
•					
○					
■					
✚					
△					
◆					
=					
✖					
★					
⊙					
◲					
#					
▼					
☐					
☐					
▽					
→					
☾					

Floss Chart

	STRAND	TYPE	NUMBER	COLOR	ALTERNATE
•					
○					
■					
✚					
△					
◆					
=					
✖					
★					
⊙					
▣					
#					
▼					
☐					
☐					
▽					
→					
☽					

80 X 100
Stitch Count

10-Square Graph Grids

Floss Chart

	STRAND	TYPE	NUMBER	COLOR	ALTERNATE
•					
○					
■					
✛					
△					
◆					
=					
✖					
★					
⊙					
▣					
#					
▼					
☐					
☐					
▽					
→					
☽					

CROSS STITCH & NEEDLEPOINT CHART AND PATTERN SKETCHBOOK

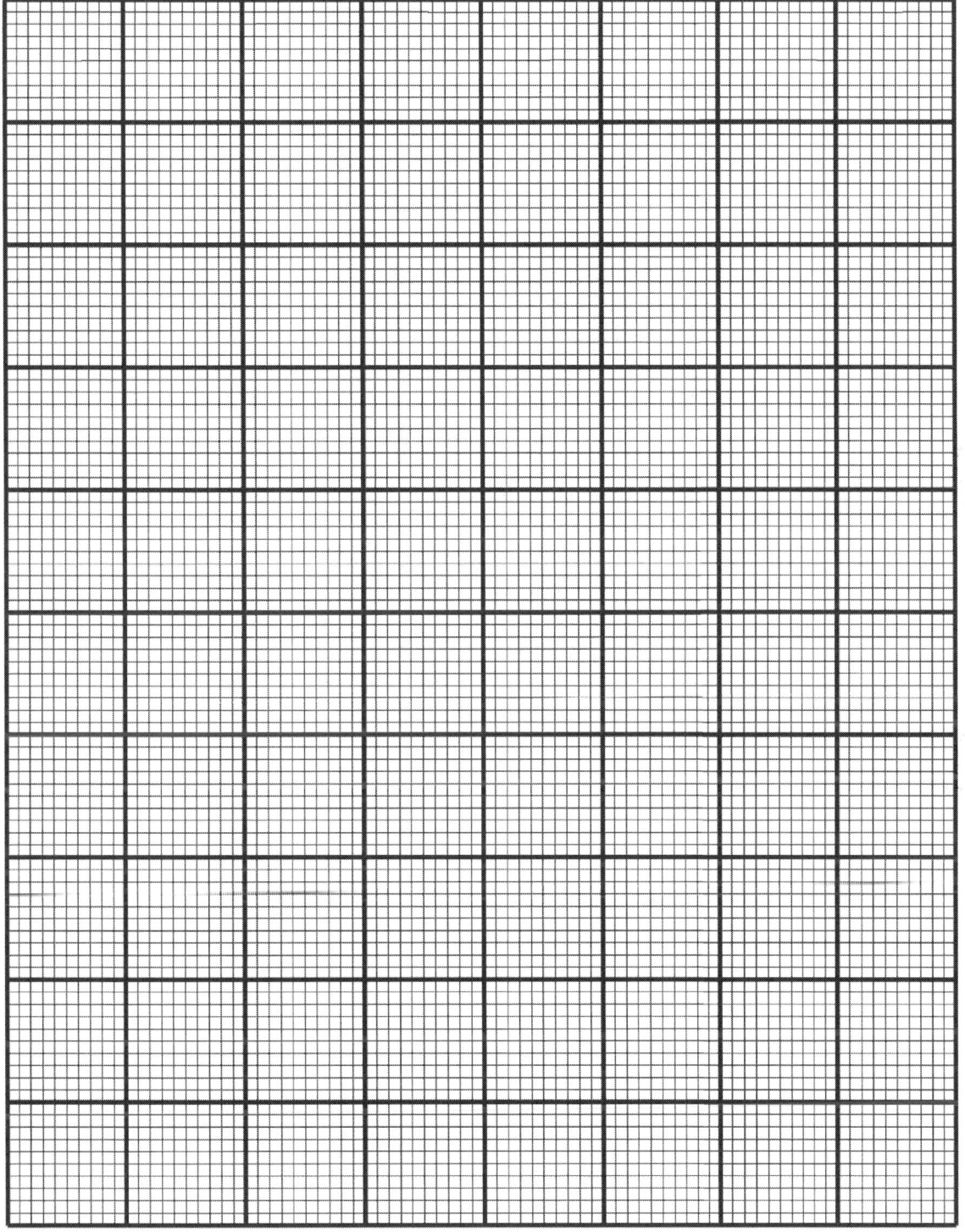

Floss Chart

	STRAND	TYPE	NUMBER	COLOR	ALTERNATE
•					
○					
■					
✚					
△					
◆					
=					
✖					
★					
⊙					
▣					
#					
▼					
□					
□					
▽					
→					
☽					

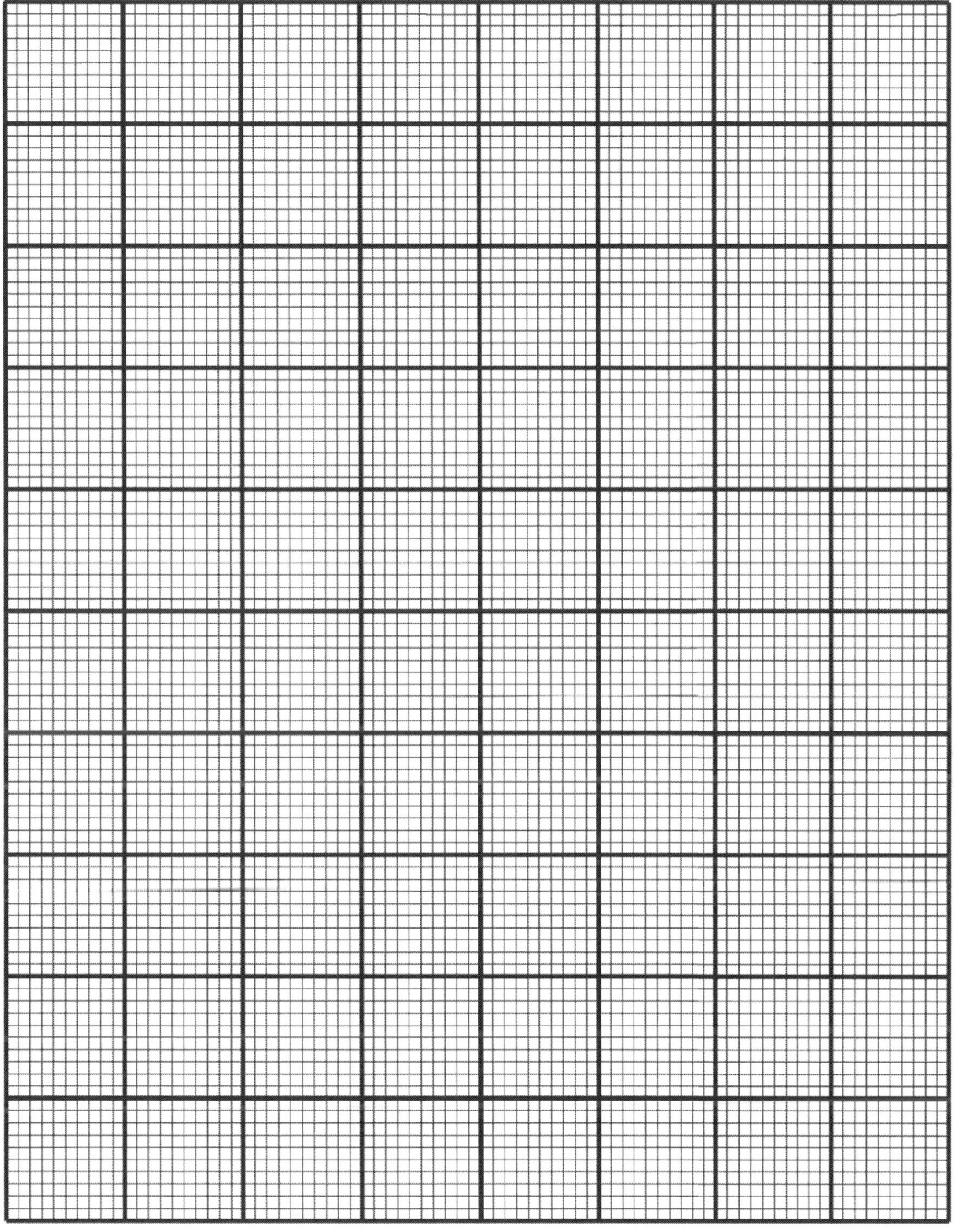

Floss Chart

	STRAND	TYPE	NUMBER	COLOR	ALTERNATE
•					
○					
■					
✚					
△					
◆					
=					
✖					
★					
⊙					
▣					
#					
▼					
□					
□					
▽					
→					
☽					

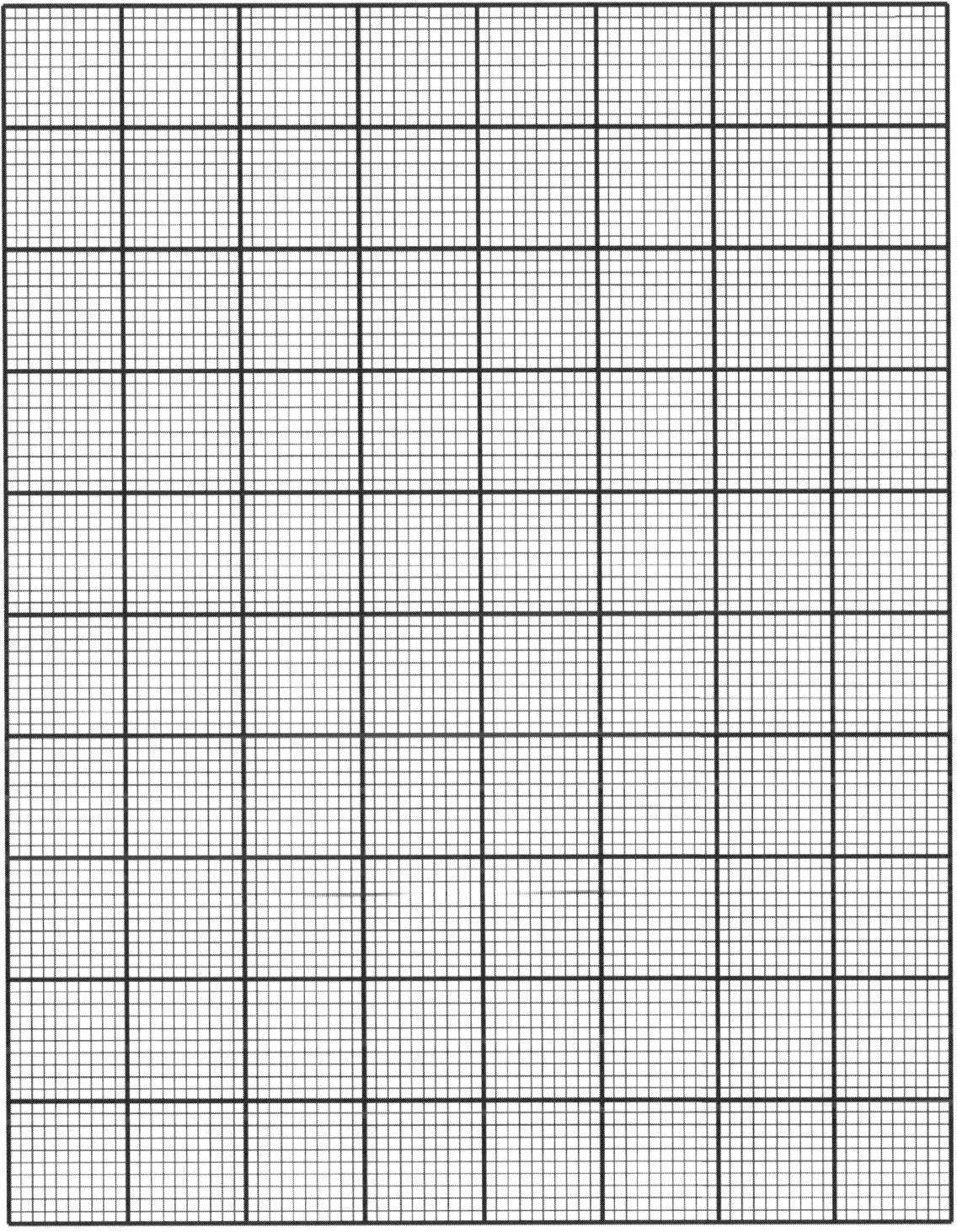

Floss Chart

	STRAND	TYPE	NUMBER	COLOR	ALTERNATE
•					
○					
■					
✚					
△					
◆					
=					
✖					
★					
⊙					
◫					
#					
▼					
☐					
☐					
▽					
→					
☾					

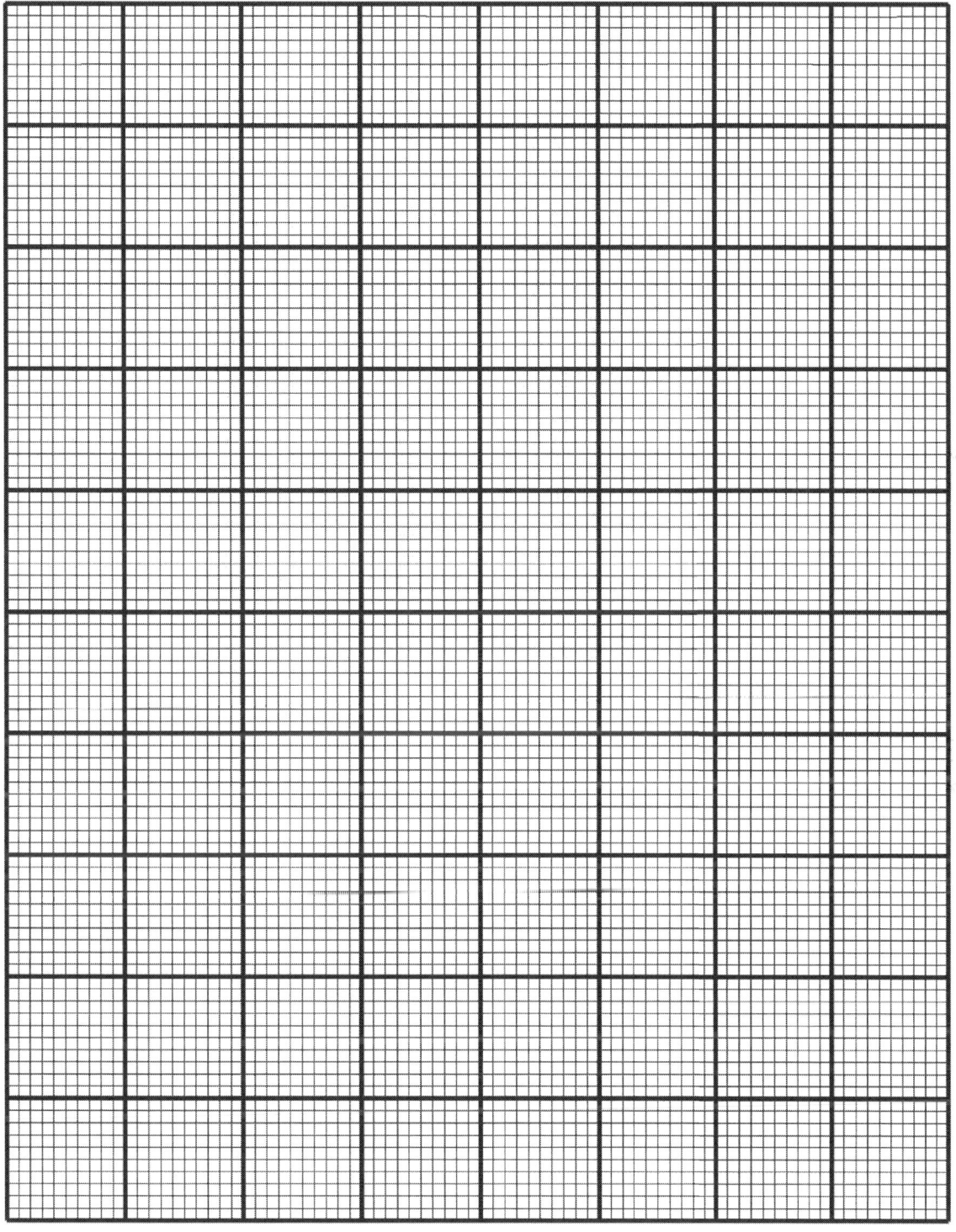

Floss Chart

	STRAND	TYPE	NUMBER	COLOR	ALTERNATE
•					
○					
■					
✚					
△					
◆					
=					
✖					
★					
⊙					
▣					
#					
▼					
☐					
☐					
▽					
→					
☾					

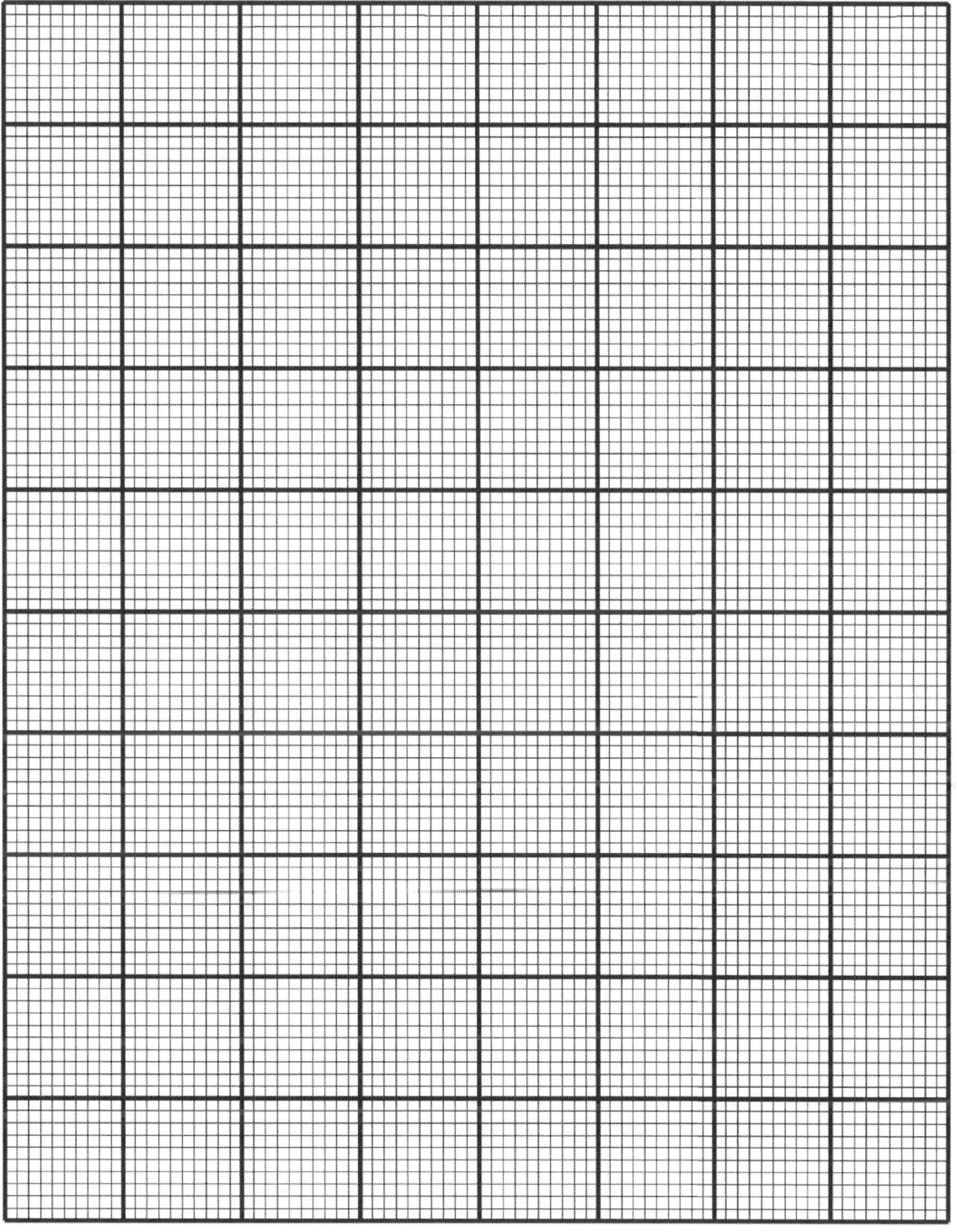

Floss Chart

	STRAND	TYPE	NUMBER	COLOR	ALTERNATE
•					
○					
■					
✚					
△					
◆					
=					
✖					
★					
⊙					
▣					
#					
▼					
▢					
▢					
▽					
→					
☽					

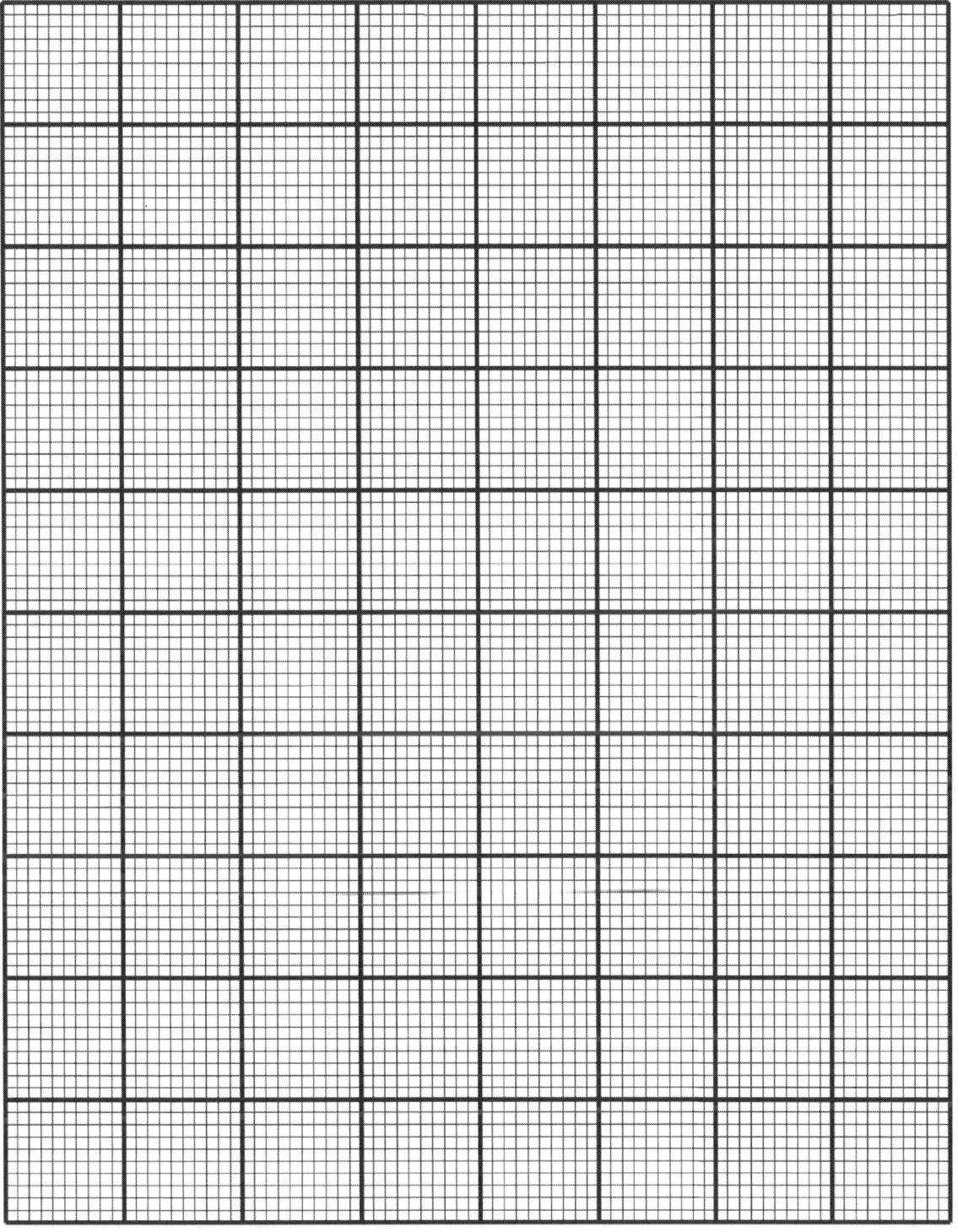

Floss Chart

	STRAND	TYPE	NUMBER	COLOR	ALTERNATE
•					
○					
■					
✚					
△					
◆					
=					
✖					
★					
⊙					
▫					
#					
▼					
□					
□					
▽					
→					
☽					

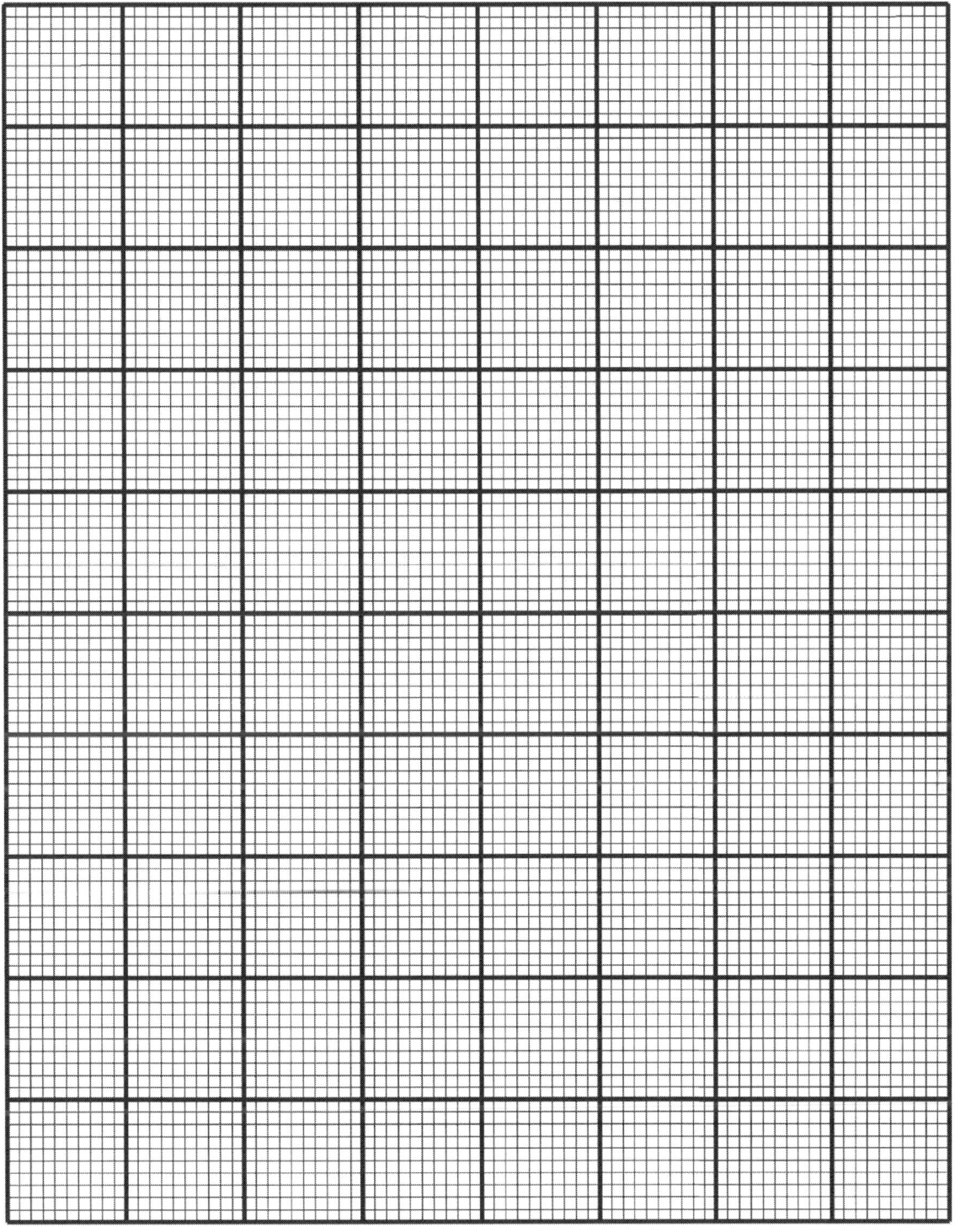

Floss Chart

	STRAND	TYPE	NUMBER	COLOR	ALTERNATE
•					
○					
■					
✚					
△					
◆					
=					
✖					
★					
⊙					
▫					
#					
▼					
☐					
☐					
▽					
→					
☾					

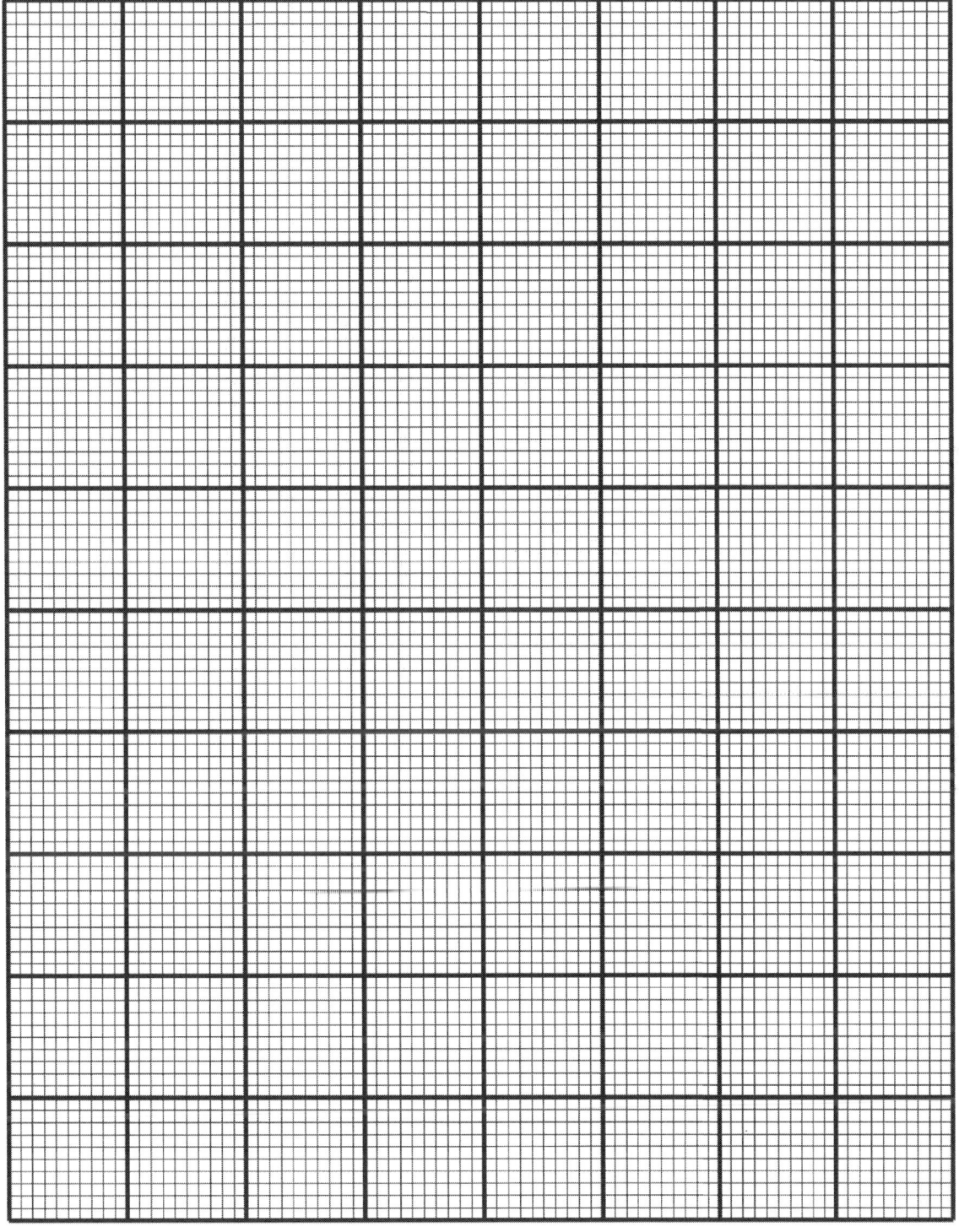

Floss Chart

	STRAND	TYPE	NUMBER	COLOR	ALTERNATE
•					
○					
■					
✚					
△					
◆					
=					
✖					
★					
⊙					
▣					
#					
▼					
☐					
☐					
▽					
→					
☽					

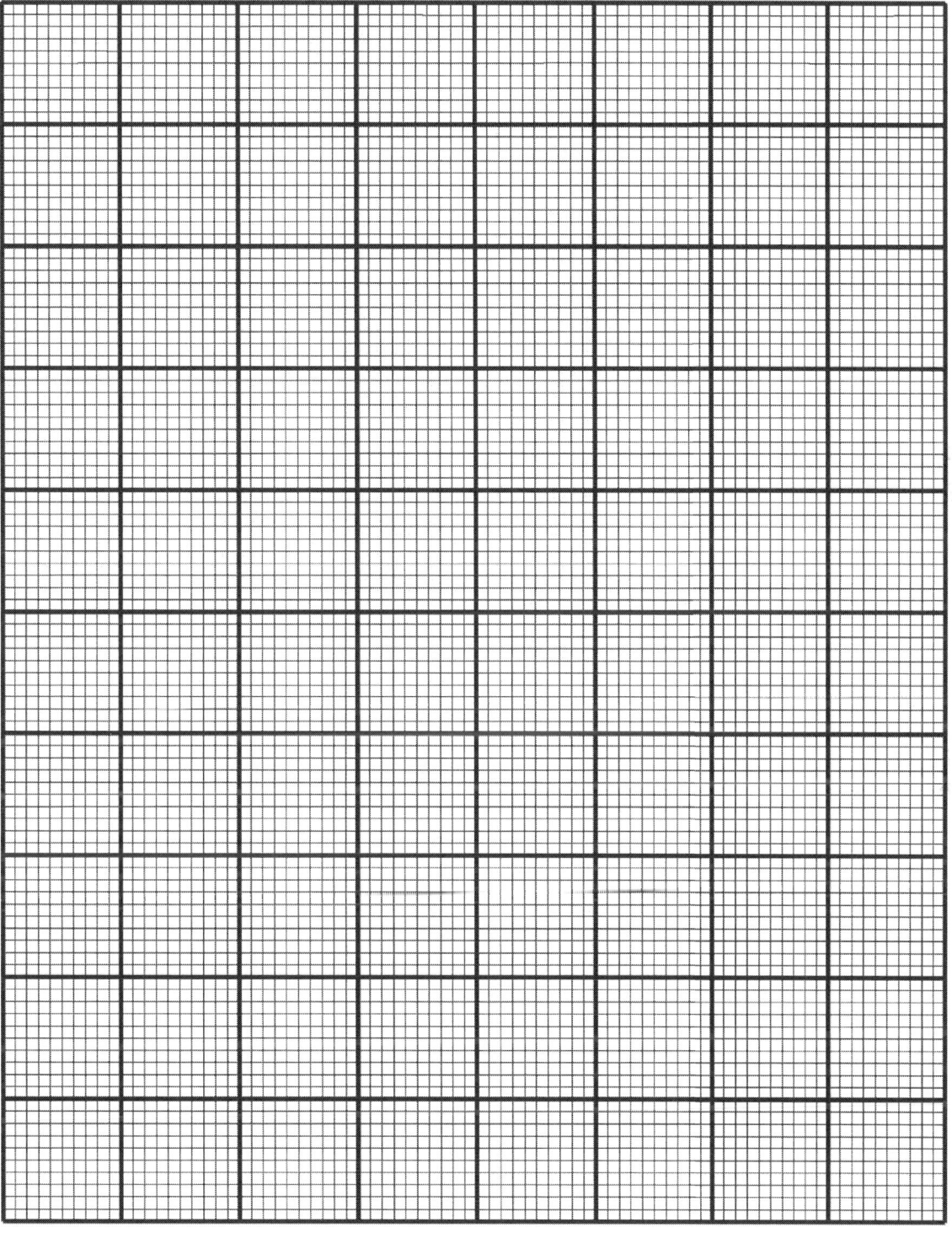

Floss Chart

	STRAND	TYPE	NUMBER	COLOR	ALTERNATE
•					
○					
■					
✚					
△					
◆					
=					
✖					
★					
⊙					
◱					
#					
▼					
☐					
☐					
▽					
→					
☾					

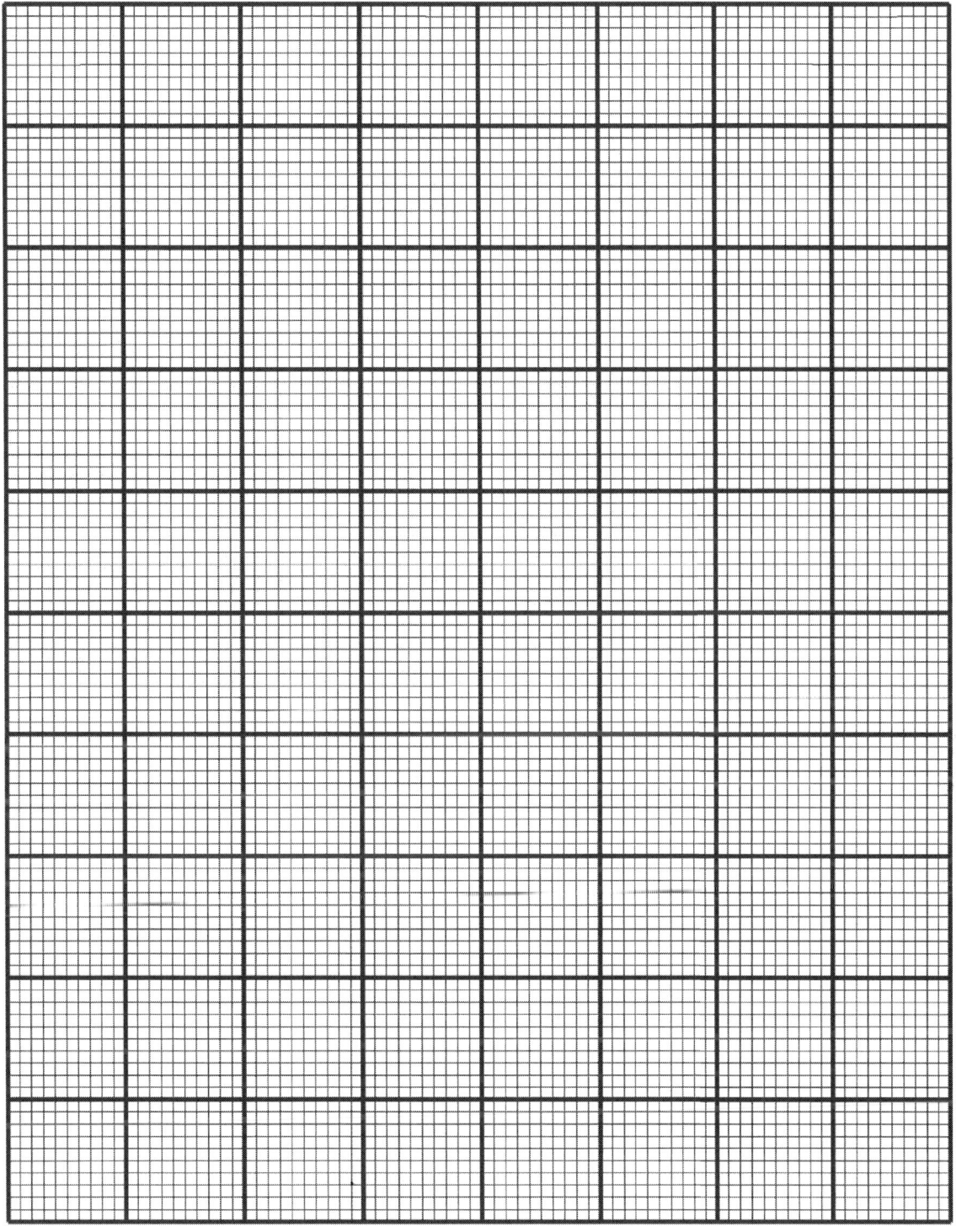

Floss Chart

	STRAND	TYPE	NUMBER	COLOR	ALTERNATE
•					
○					
■					
✚					
△					
◆					
=					
✖					
★					
⊙					
▣					
#					
▼					
☐					
☐					
▽					
→					
☽					

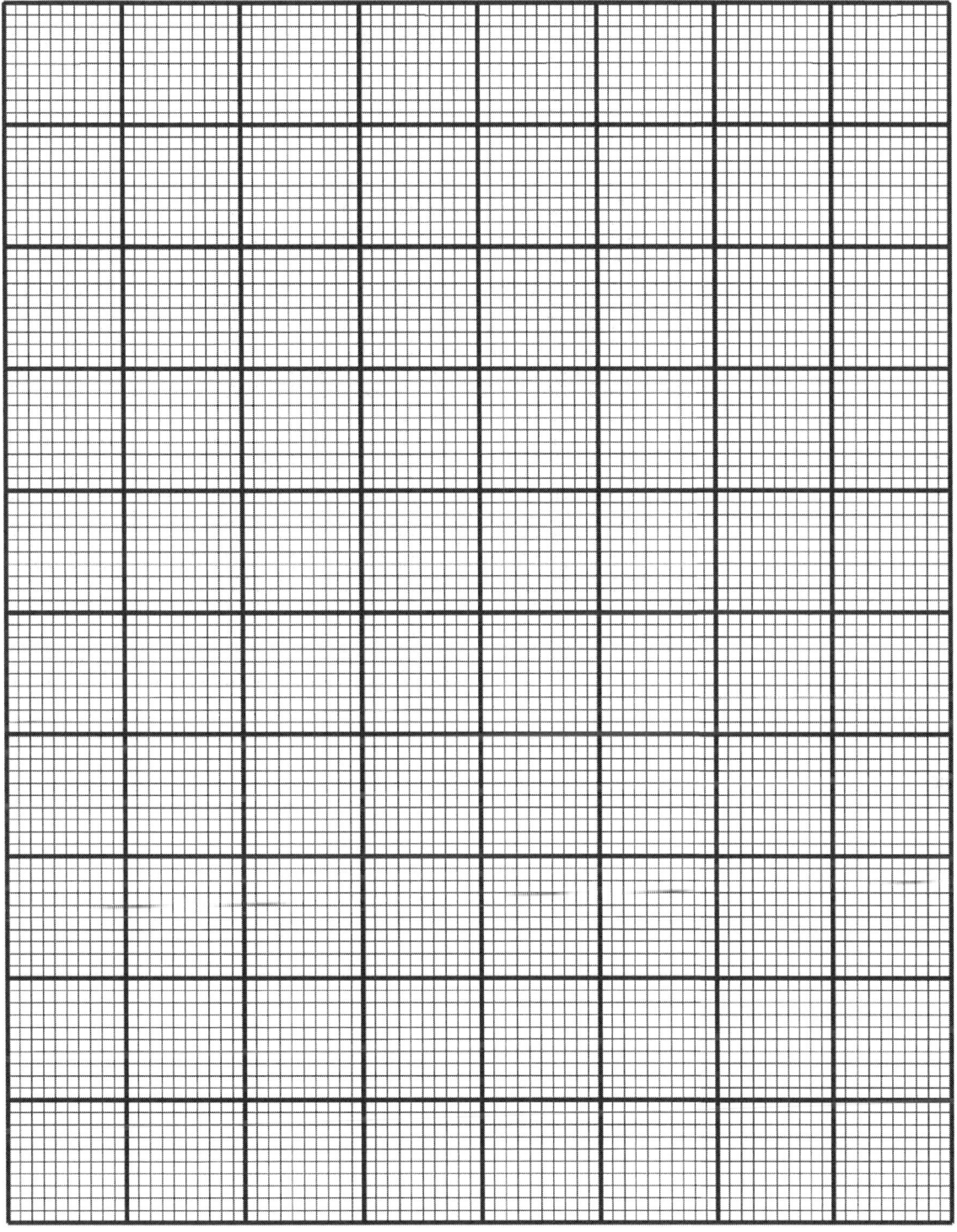

Floss Chart

	STRAND	TYPE	NUMBER	COLOR	ALTERNATE
•					
○					
■					
✚					
△					
◆					
=					
✖					
★					
⊙					
▫					
#					
▼					
▢					
▢					
▽					
→					
☽					

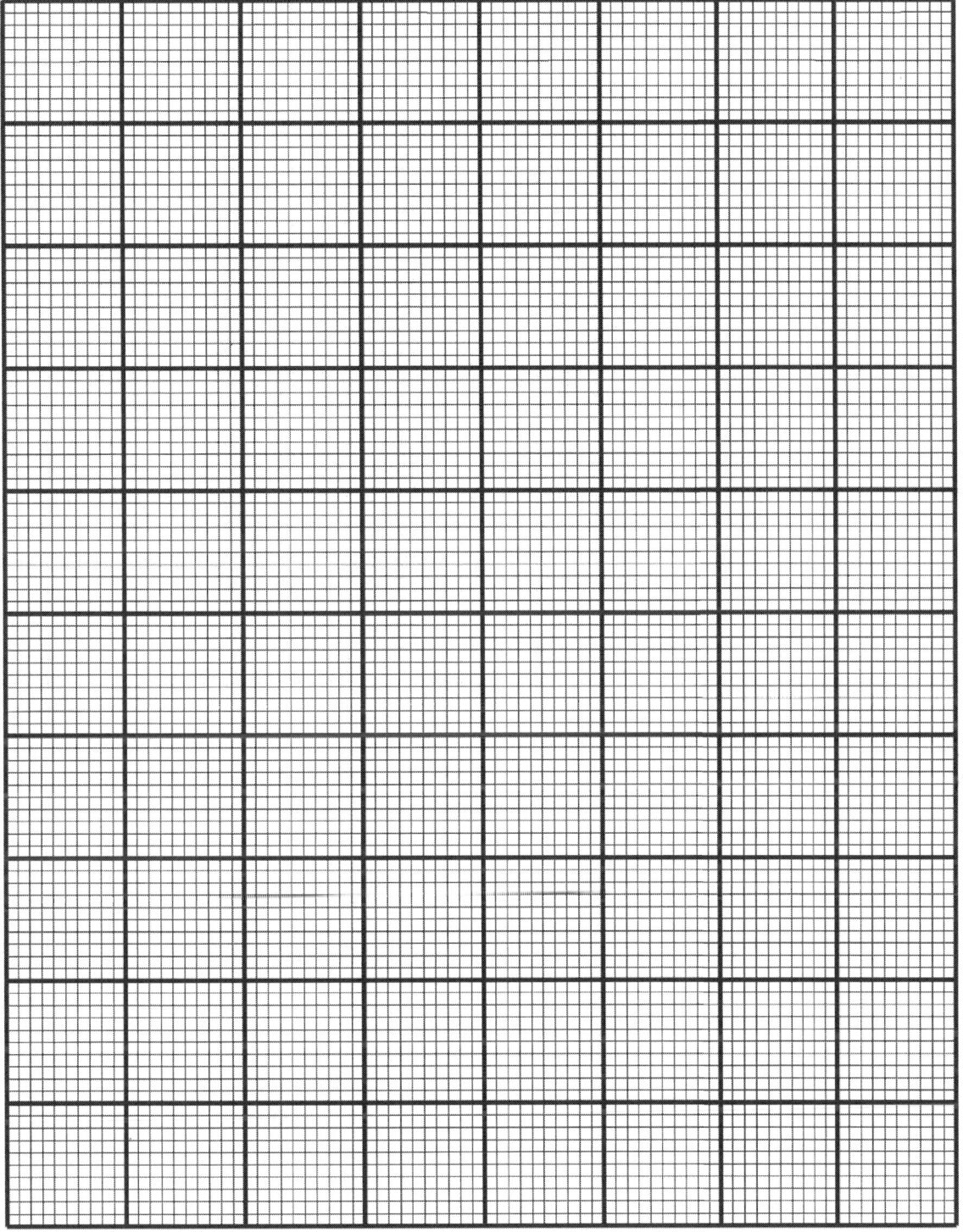

Floss Chart

STRAND	TYPE	NUMBER	COLOR	ALTERNATE
•				
○				
■				
✚				
△				
◆				
=				
✖				
★				
⊙				
▫				
#				
▼				
☐				
☐				
▽				
→				
☽				

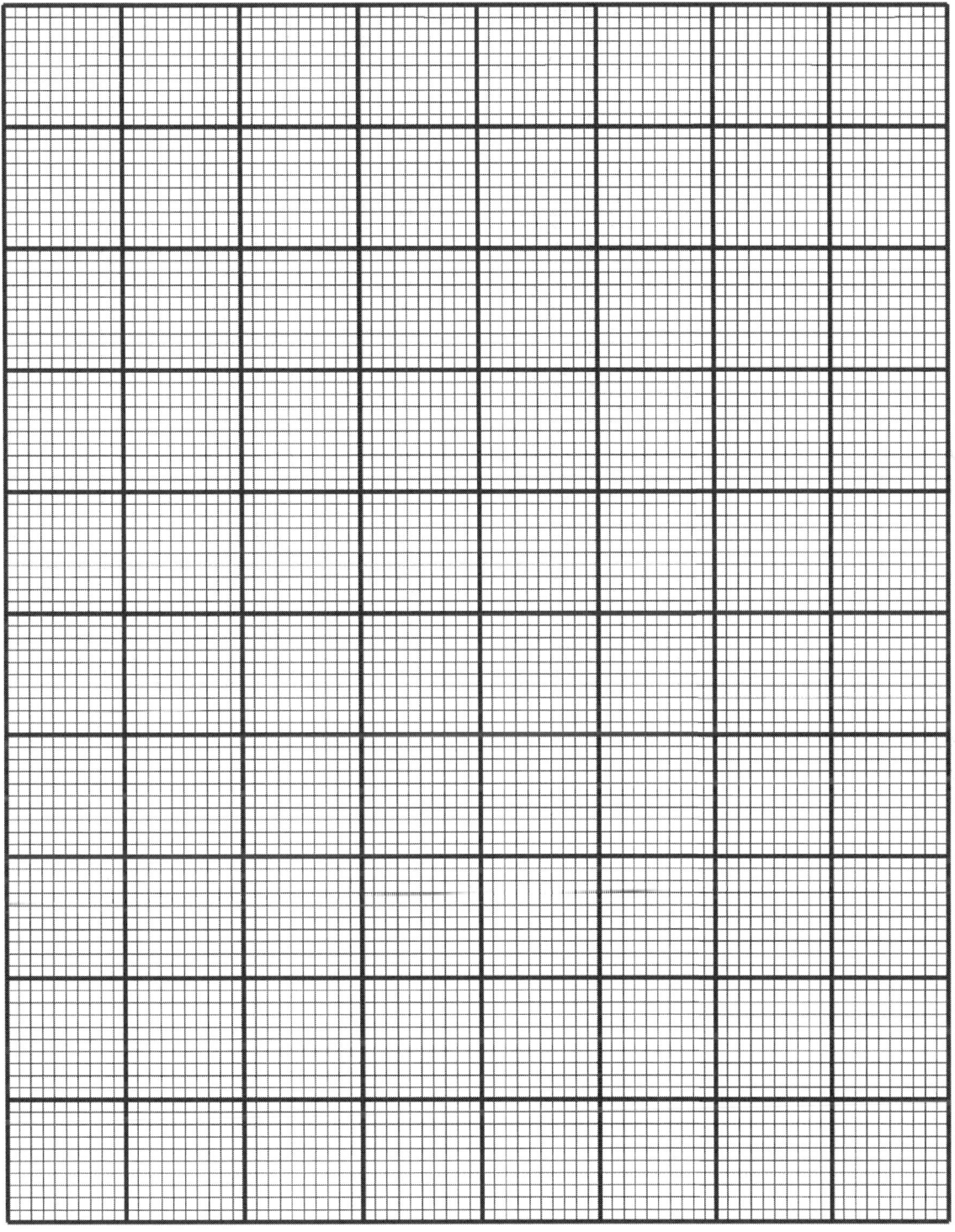

Floss Chart

	STRAND	TYPE	NUMBER	COLOR	ALTERNATE
•					
○					
■					
✚					
△					
◆					
=					
✖					
★					
⊙					
▣					
#					
▼					
☐					
☐					
▽					
→					
☾					

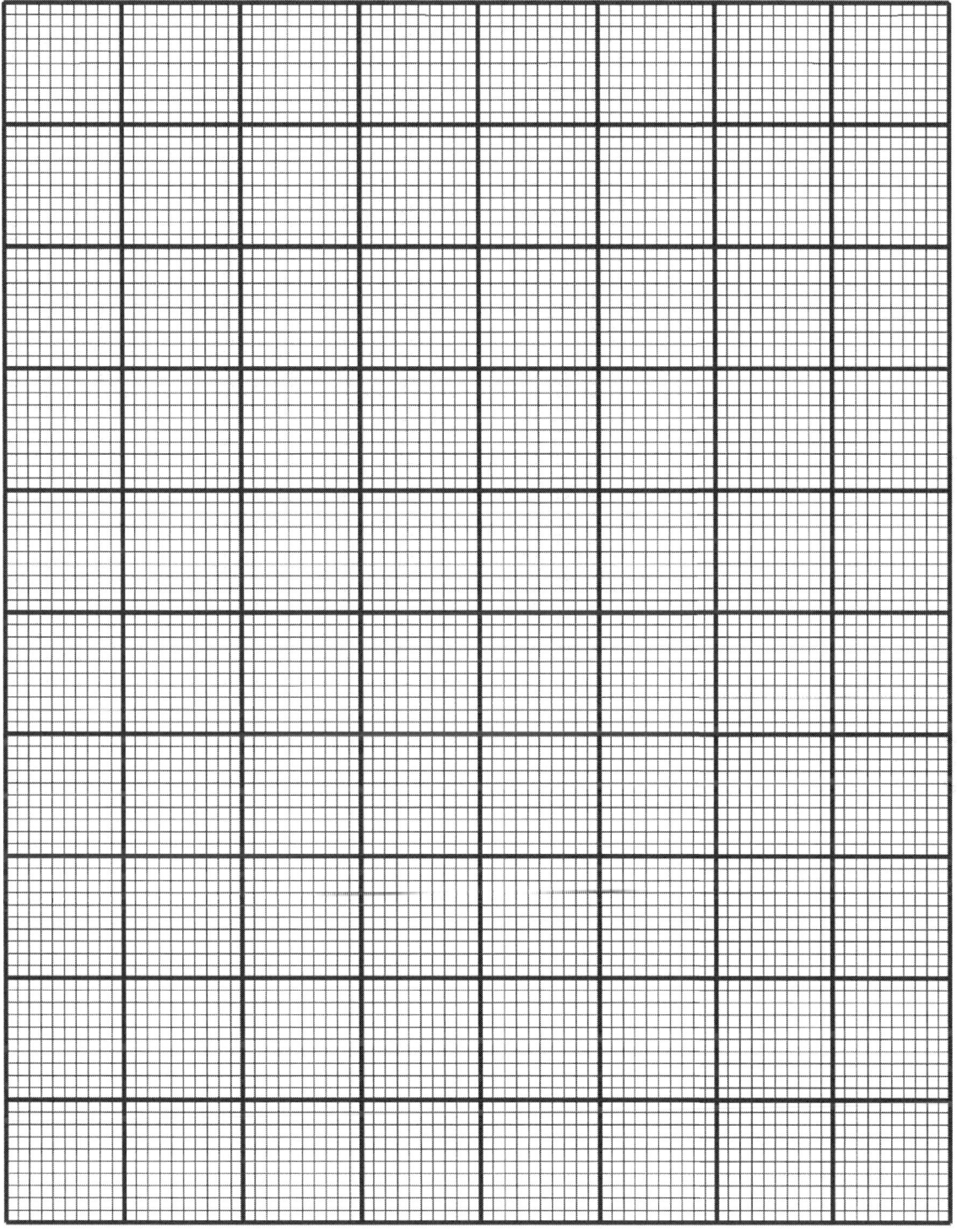

Floss Chart

	STRAND	TYPE	NUMBER	COLOR	ALTERNATE
•					
○					
■					
✚					
△					
◆					
=					
✖					
★					
⊙					
◫					
#					
▼					
□					
□					
▽					
→					
☽					

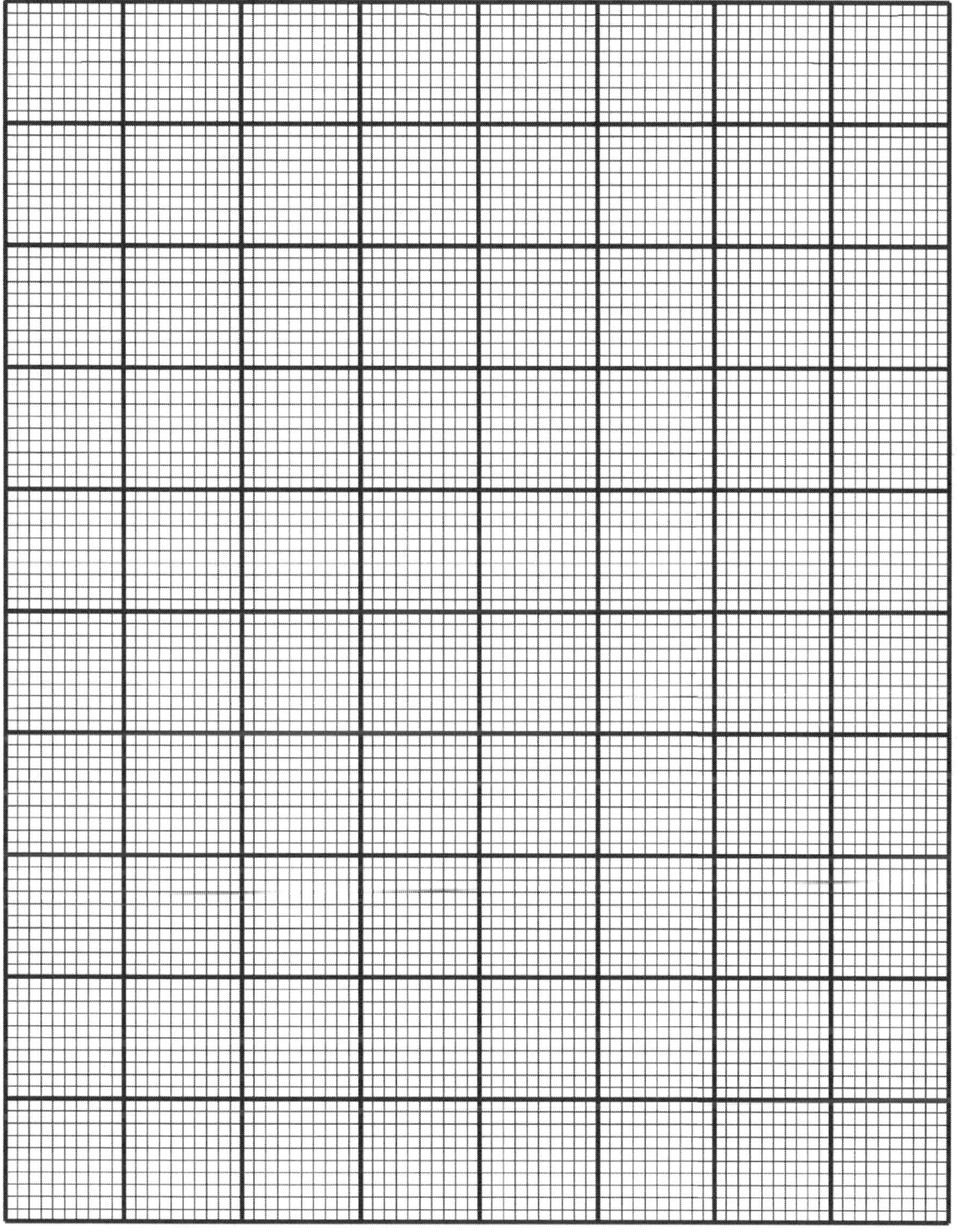

Floss Chart

	STRAND	TYPE	NUMBER	COLOR	ALTERNATE
•					
○					
■					
✚					
△					
◆					
=					
✖					
★					
⊙					
▫					
#					
▼					
□					
□					
▽					
→					
☾					

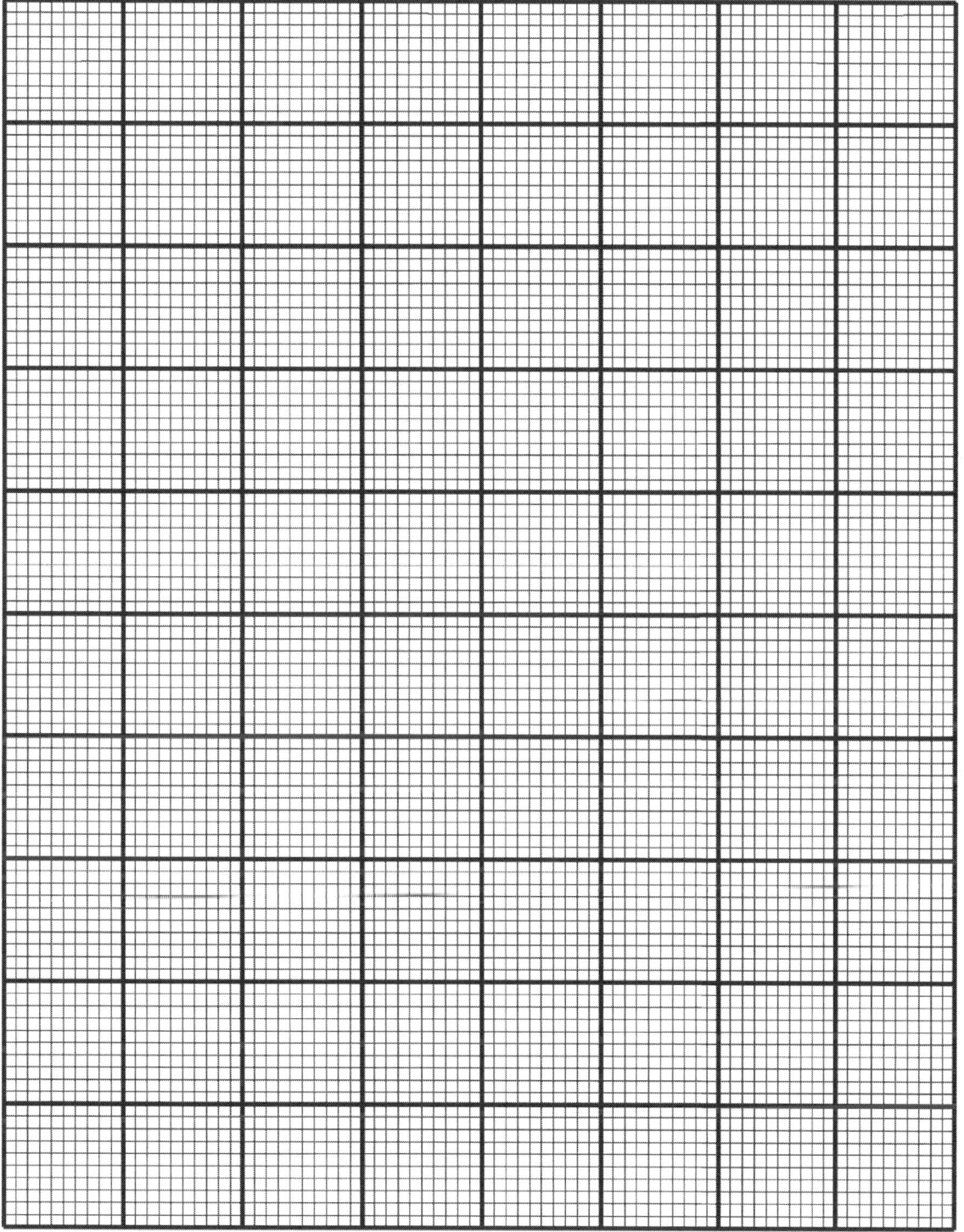

Floss Chart

Symbol	STRAND	TYPE	NUMBER	COLOR	ALTERNATE
•					
○					
■					
✚					
△					
◆					
=					
✖					
★					
⊙					
▫					
#					
▼					
□					
□					
▽					
→					
☽					

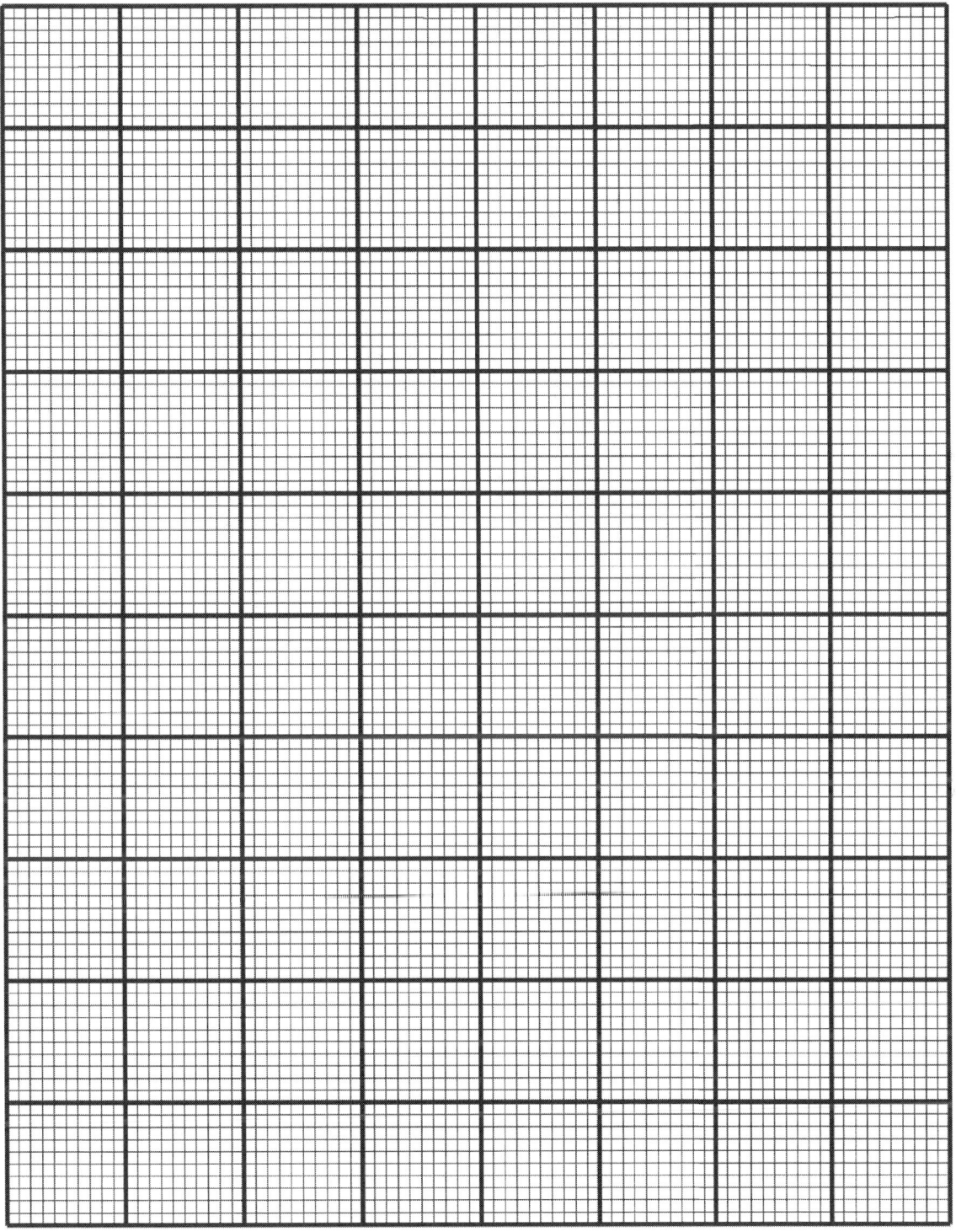

Floss Chart

	STRAND	TYPE	NUMBER	COLOR	ALTERNATE
•					
○					
■					
✚					
△					
◆					
=					
✖					
★					
⊙					
▣					
#					
▼					
□					
□					
▽					
→					
☽					

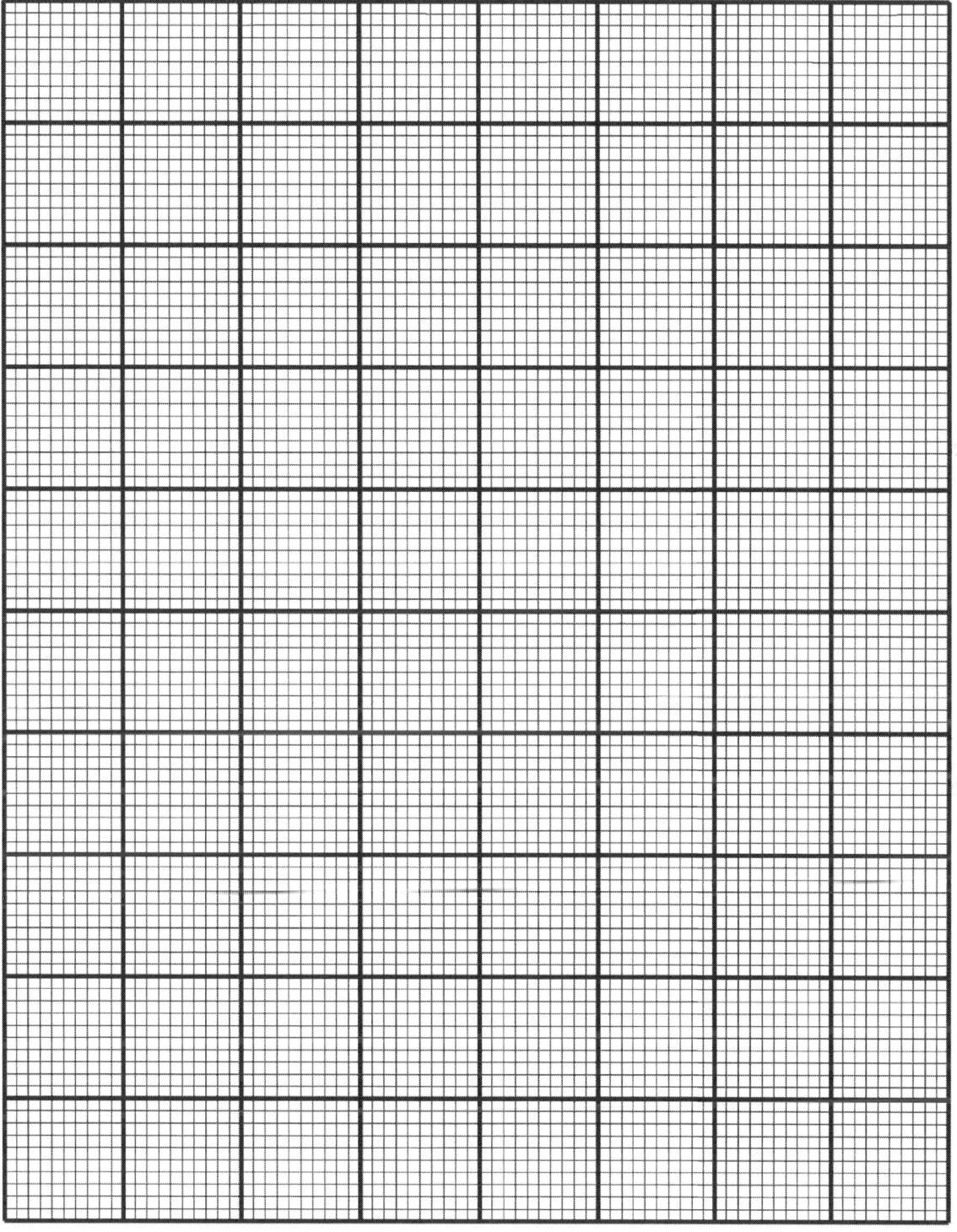

Floss Chart

	STRAND	TYPE	NUMBER	COLOR	ALTERNATE
•					
○					
■					
✚					
△					
◆					
=					
✖					
★					
⊙					
▫					
#					
▼					
☐					
☐					
▽					
→					
☾					

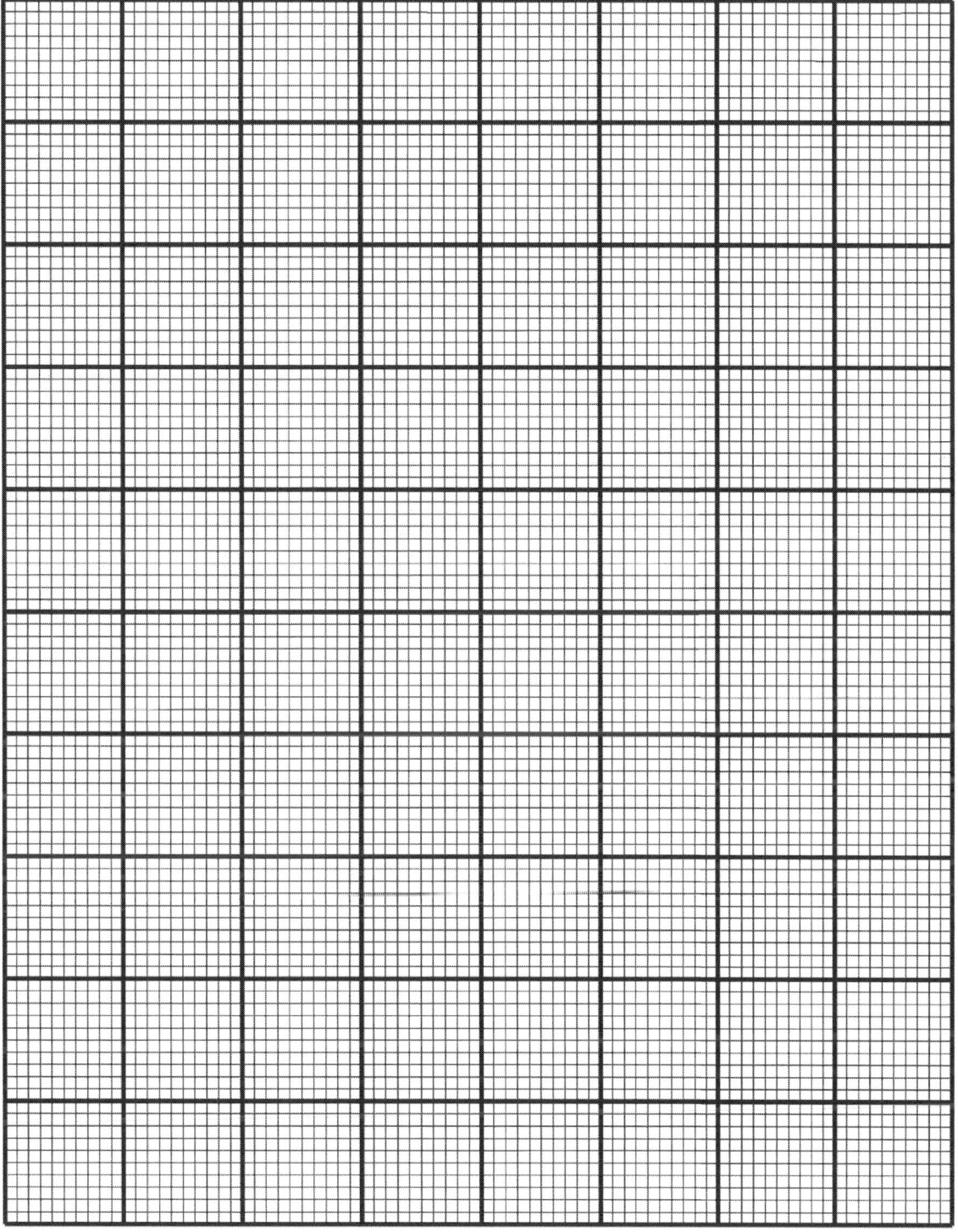

Floss Chart

	STRAND	TYPE	NUMBER	COLOR	ALTERNATE
•					
○					
■					
✚					
△					
◆					
=					
✖					
★					
⊙					
◳					
#					
▼					
◻					
◻					
▽					
→					
☾					

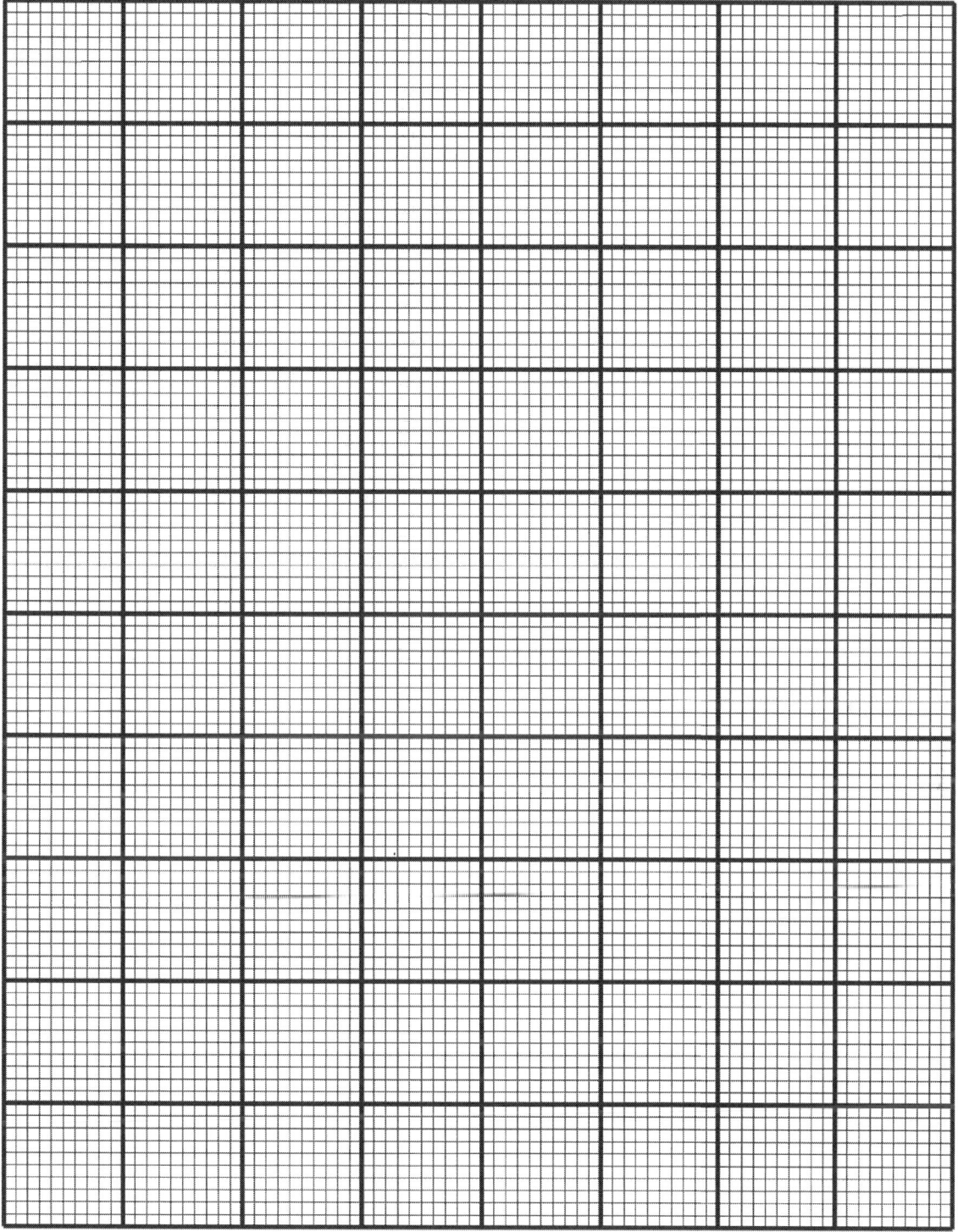

60 X 80 Stitch Count

10-Square Graph Grids

Floss Chart

	STRAND	TYPE	NUMBER	COLOR	ALTERNATE
•					
○					
■					
✚					
△					
◆					
=					
✖					
★					
⊙					
▣					
#					
▼					
☐					
☐					
▽					
→					
☽					

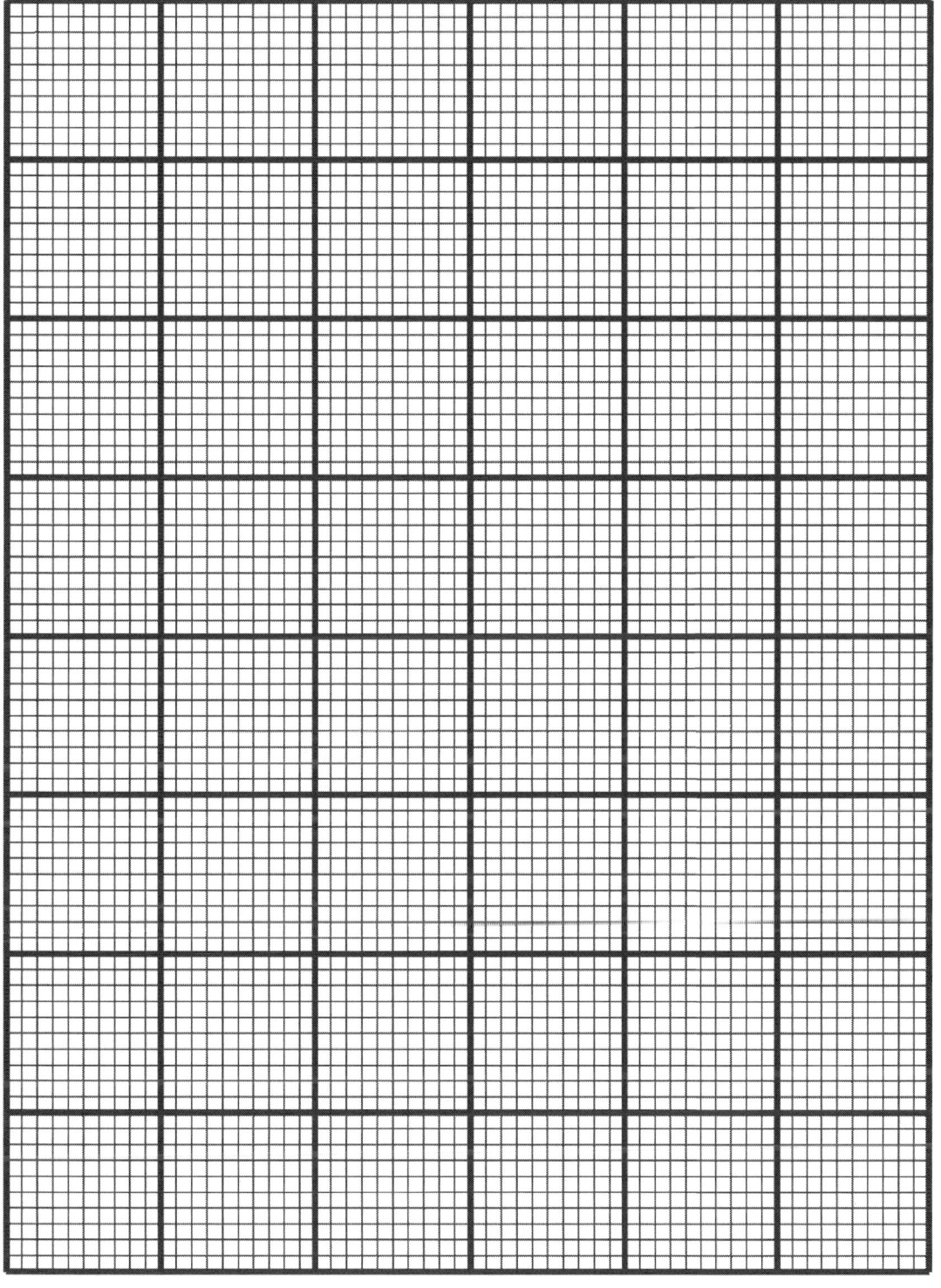

Floss Chart

	STRAND	TYPE	NUMBER	COLOR	ALTERNATE
•					
○					
■					
✚					
△					
◆					
=					
✖					
★					
⊙					
▫					
#					
▼					
☐					
☐					
▽					
→					
☽					

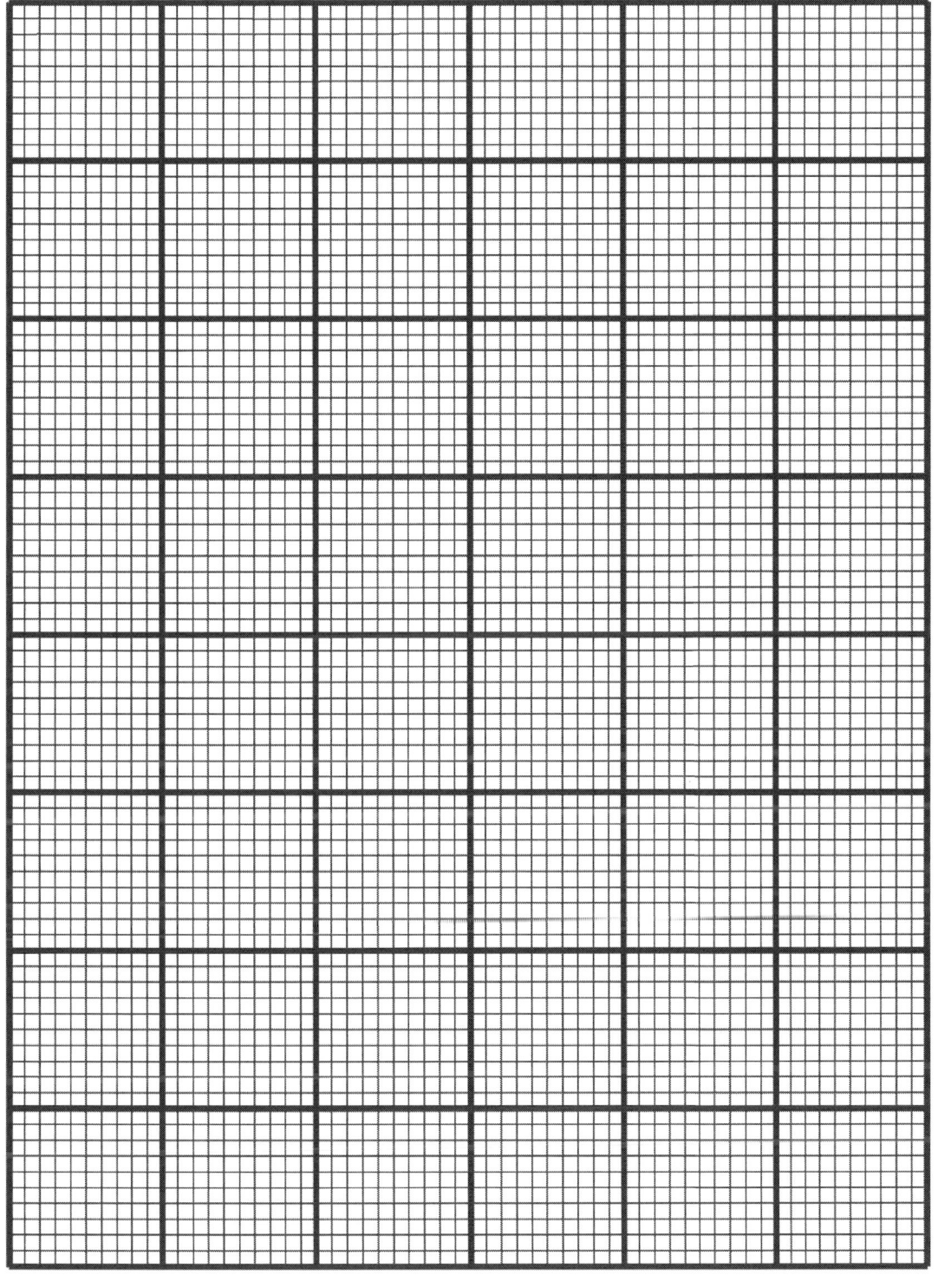

Floss Chart

	STRAND	TYPE	NUMBER	COLOR	ALTERNATE
•					
○					
■					
✚					
△					
◆					
=					
✖					
★					
⊙					
▣					
#					
▼					
☐					
☐					
▽					
→					
☾					

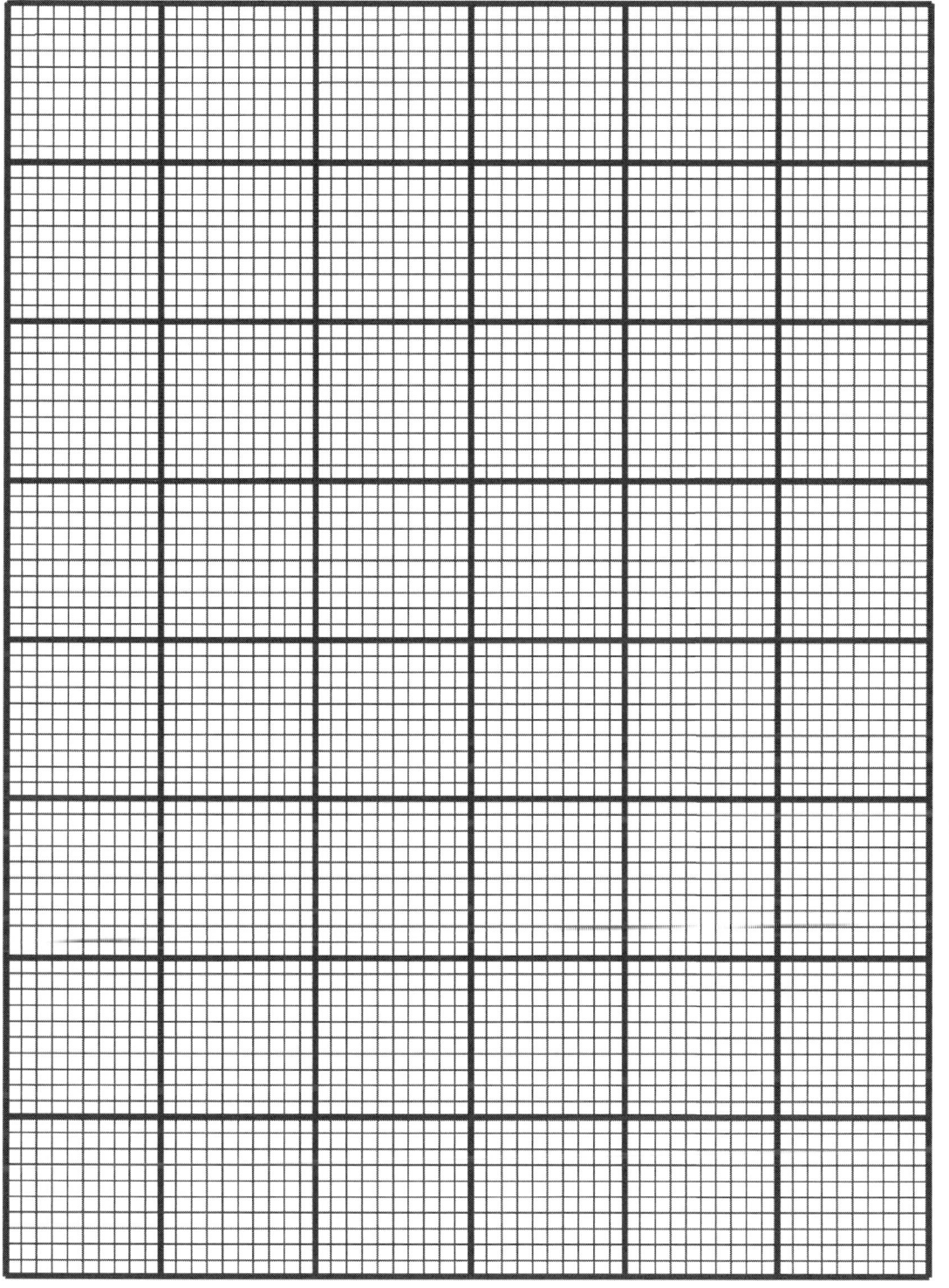

Floss Chart

	STRAND	TYPE	NUMBER	COLOR	ALTERNATE
•					
○					
■					
✚					
△					
◆					
=					
✖					
★					
⊙					
▣					
#					
▼					
□					
□					
▽					
→					
☾					

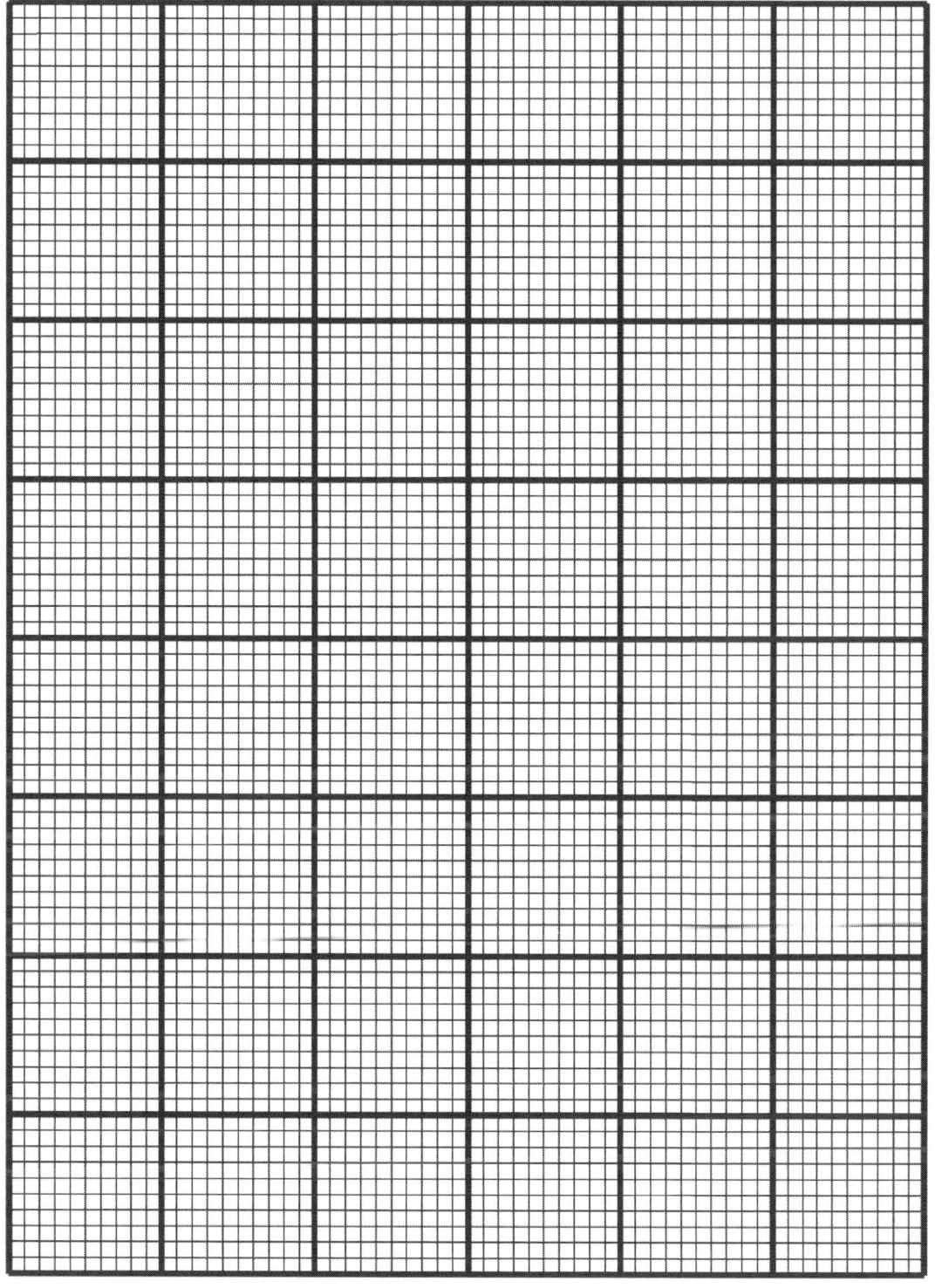

Floss Chart

	STRAND	TYPE	NUMBER	COLOR	ALTERNATE
•					
○					
■					
✚					
△					
◆					
=					
✖					
★					
⊙					
▫					
#					
▼					
☐					
☐					
▽					
→					
☾					

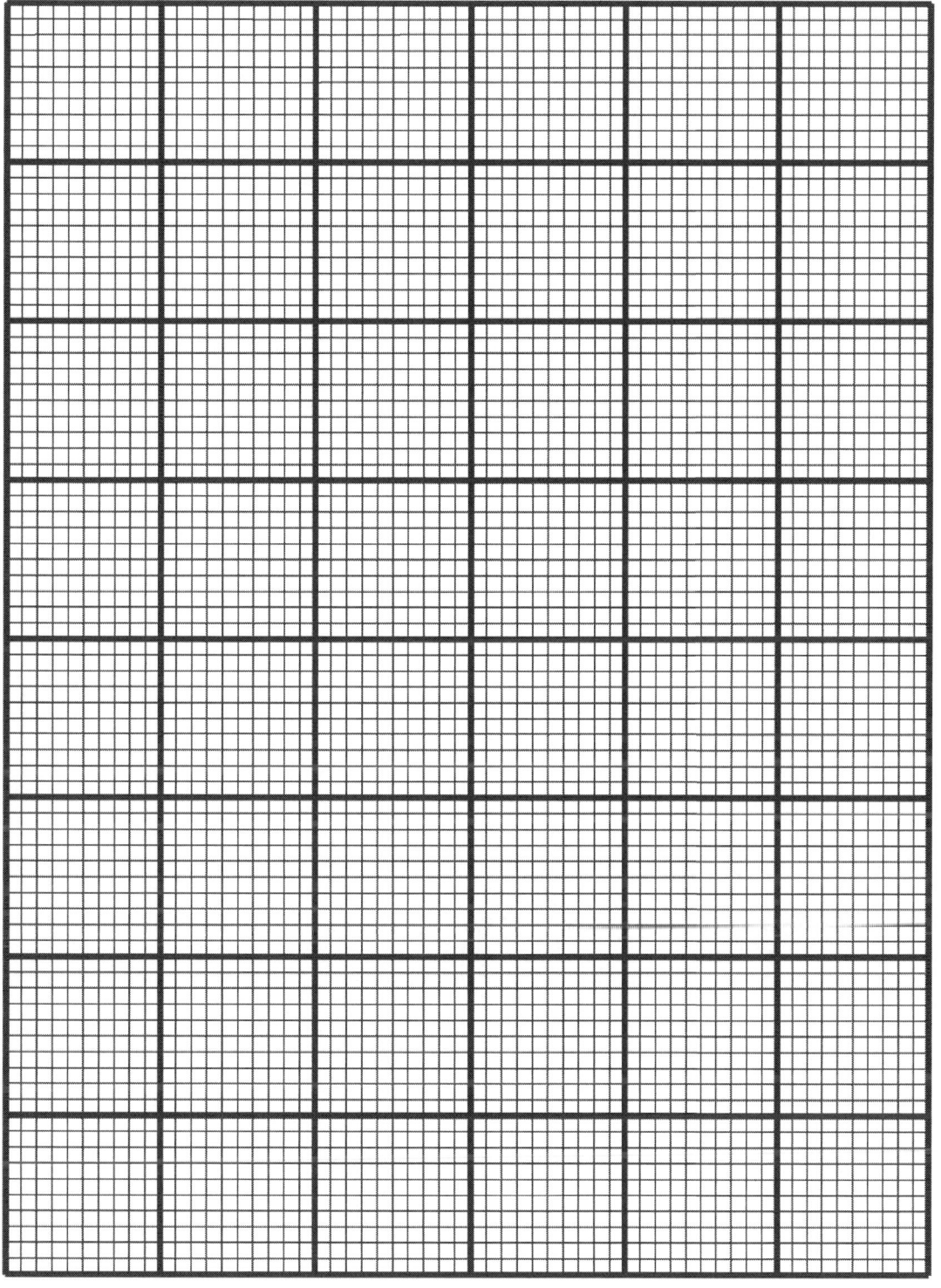

Floss Chart

	STRAND	TYPE	NUMBER	COLOR	ALTERNATE
•					
○					
■					
✚					
△					
◆					
=					
✖					
★					
⊙					
▫					
#					
▼					
□					
□					
▽					
→					
☽					

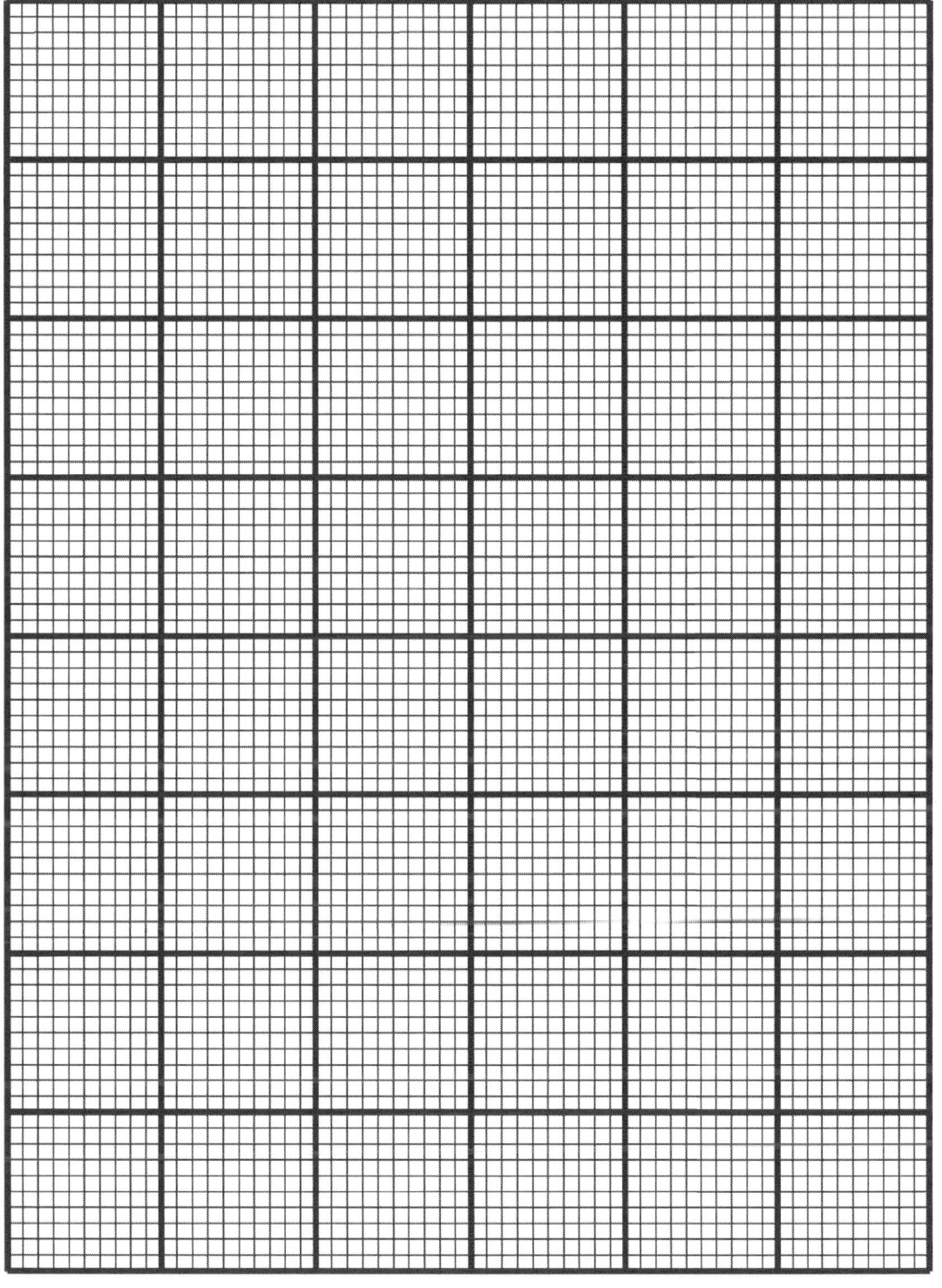

Floss Chart

Symbol	STRAND	TYPE	NUMBER	COLOR	ALTERNATE
•					
○					
■					
✚					
△					
◆					
=					
✖					
★					
⊙					
◘					
#					
▼					
☐					
☐					
▽					
→					
☾					

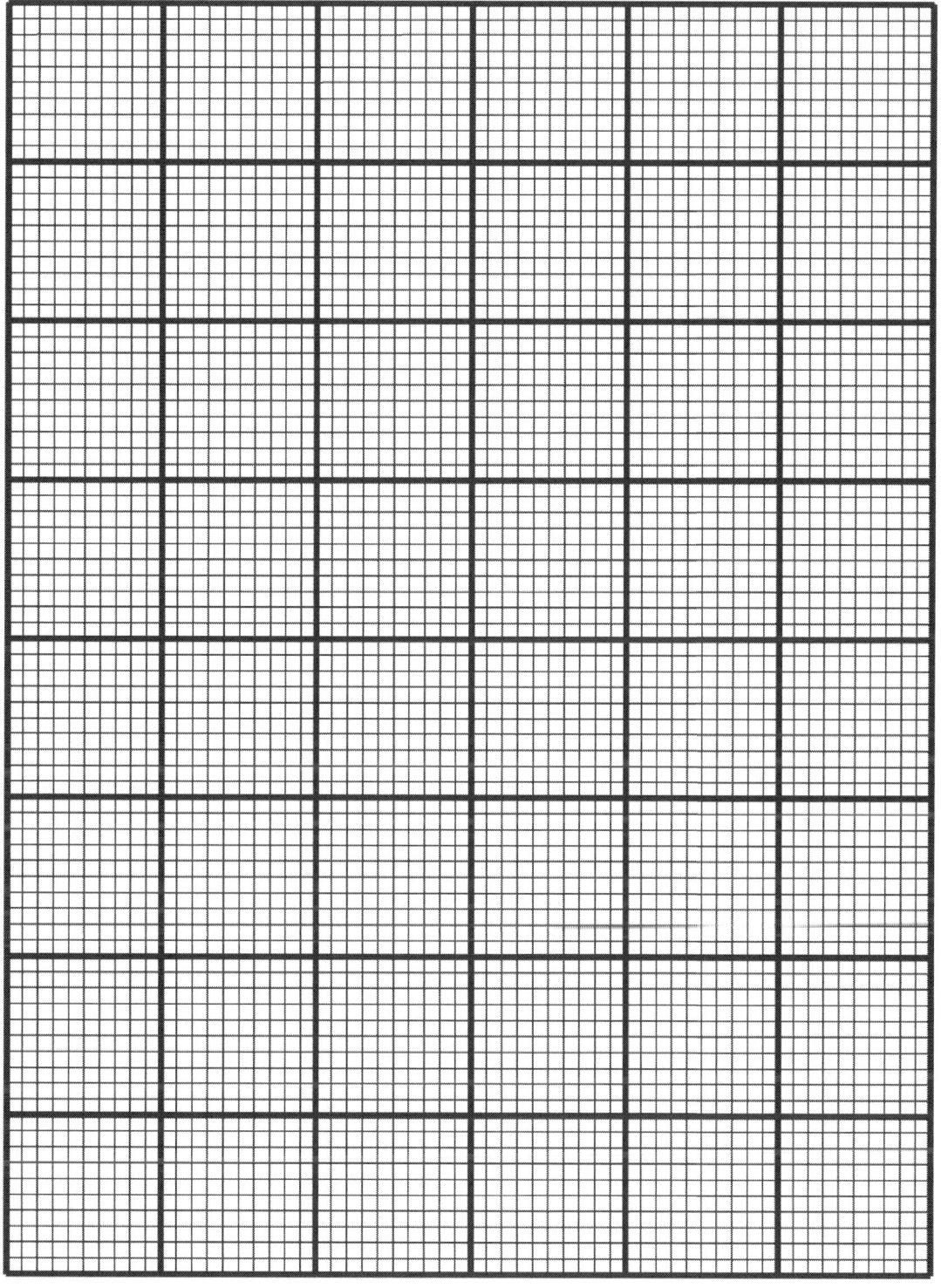

Floss Chart

	STRAND	TYPE	NUMBER	COLOR	ALTERNATE
•					
○					
■					
✚					
△					
◆					
=					
✖					
★					
⊙					
▣					
#					
▼					
☐					
☐					
▽					
→					
☾					

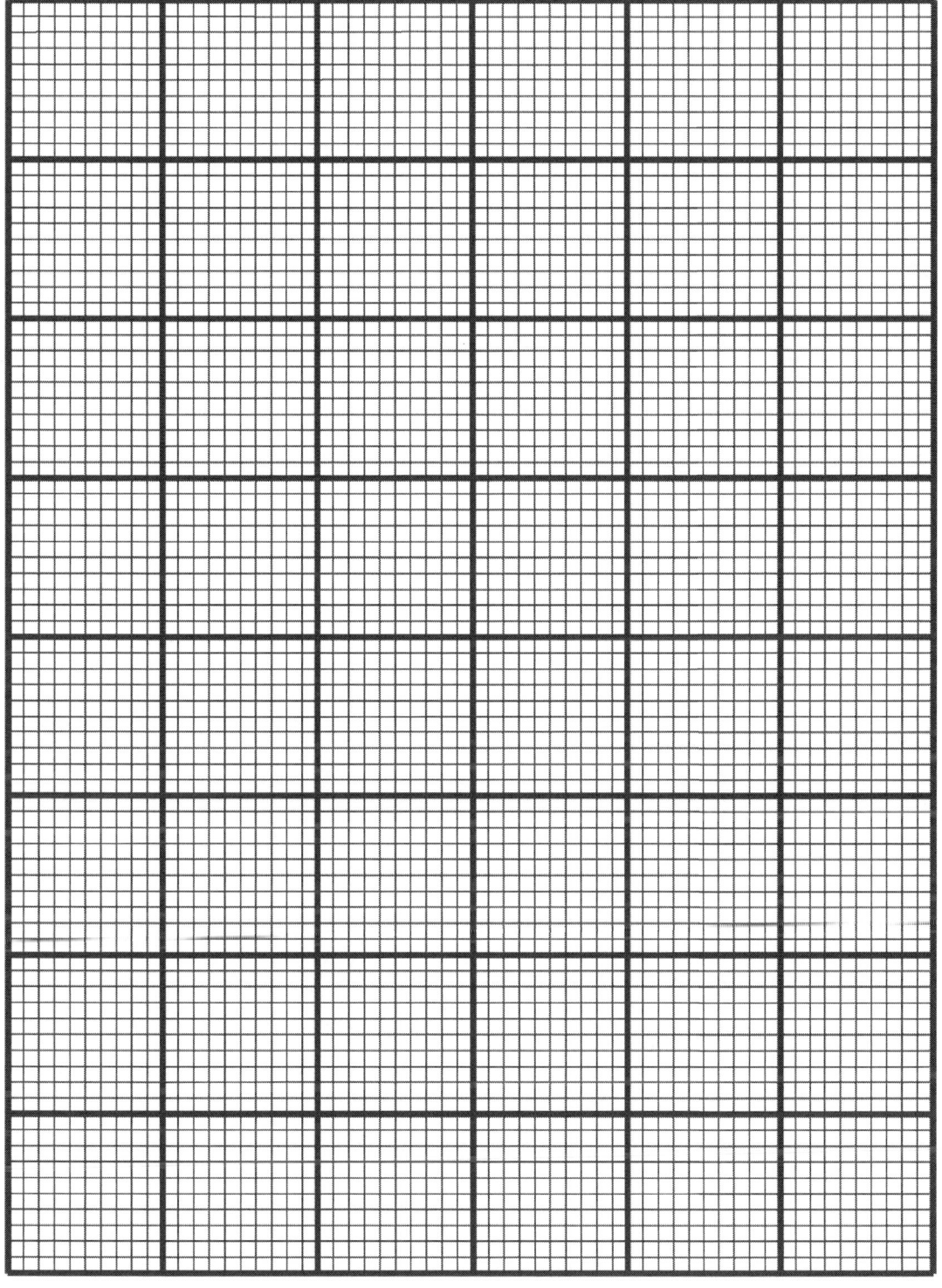

Floss Chart

	STRAND	TYPE	NUMBER	COLOR	ALTERNATE
•					
○					
■					
✚					
△					
◆					
=					
✖					
★					
⊙					
▣					
#					
▼					
☐					
☐					
▽					
→					
☽					

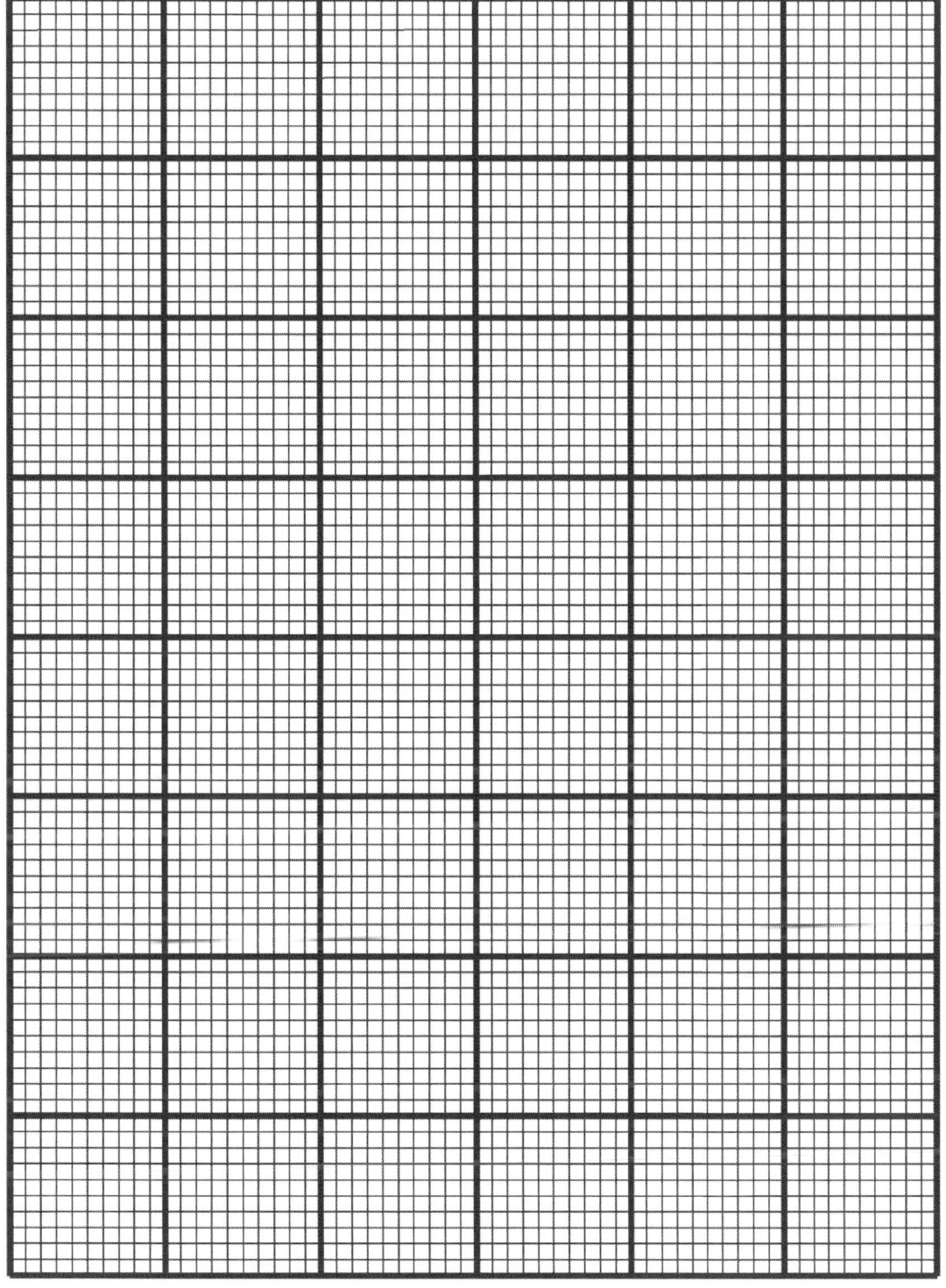

Floss Chart

	STRAND	TYPE	NUMBER	COLOR	ALTERNATE
•					
○					
■					
✚					
△					
◆					
=					
✖					
★					
⊙					
▫					
#					
▼					
□					
□					
▽					
→					
☾					

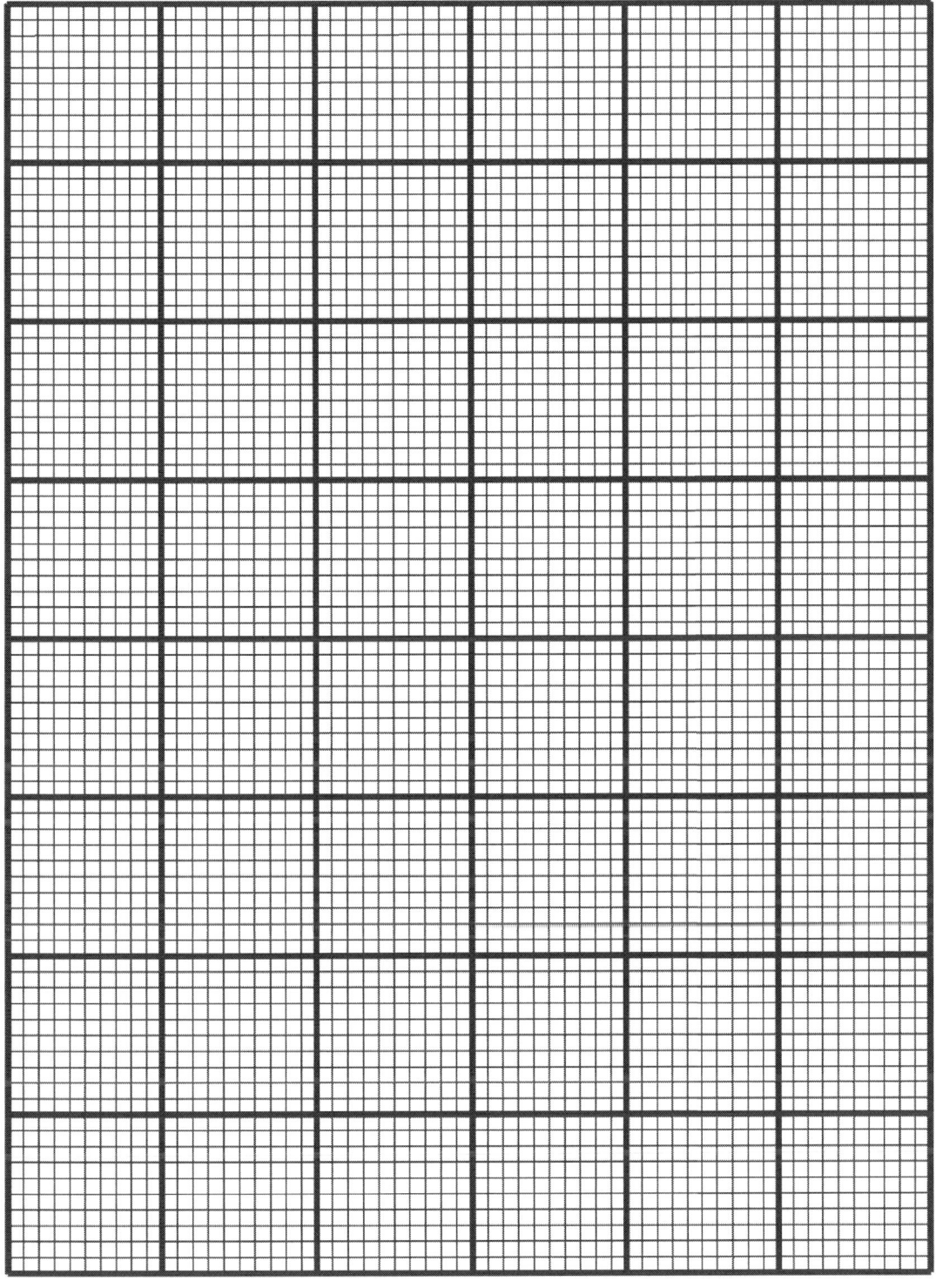

Floss Chart

	STRAND	TYPE	NUMBER	COLOR	ALTERNATE
•					
○					
■					
✚					
△					
◆					
=					
✖					
★					
⊙					
▣					
#					
▼					
☐					
☐					
▽					
→					
☾					

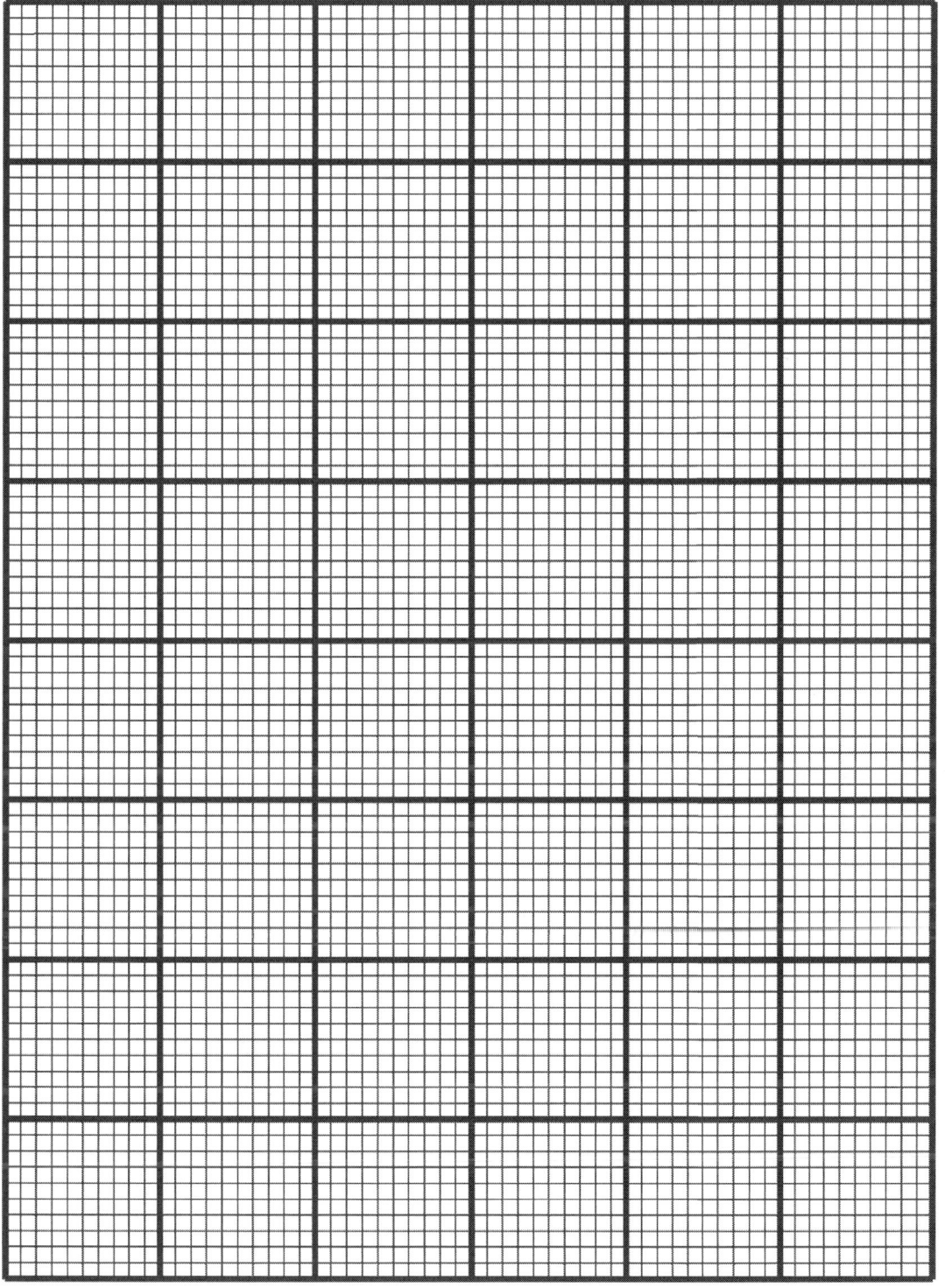

Floss Chart

	STRAND	TYPE	NUMBER	COLOR	ALTERNATE
•					
○					
■					
✚					
△					
◆					
=					
✖					
★					
⊙					
◪					
#					
▼					
☐					
☐					
▽					
→					
☾					

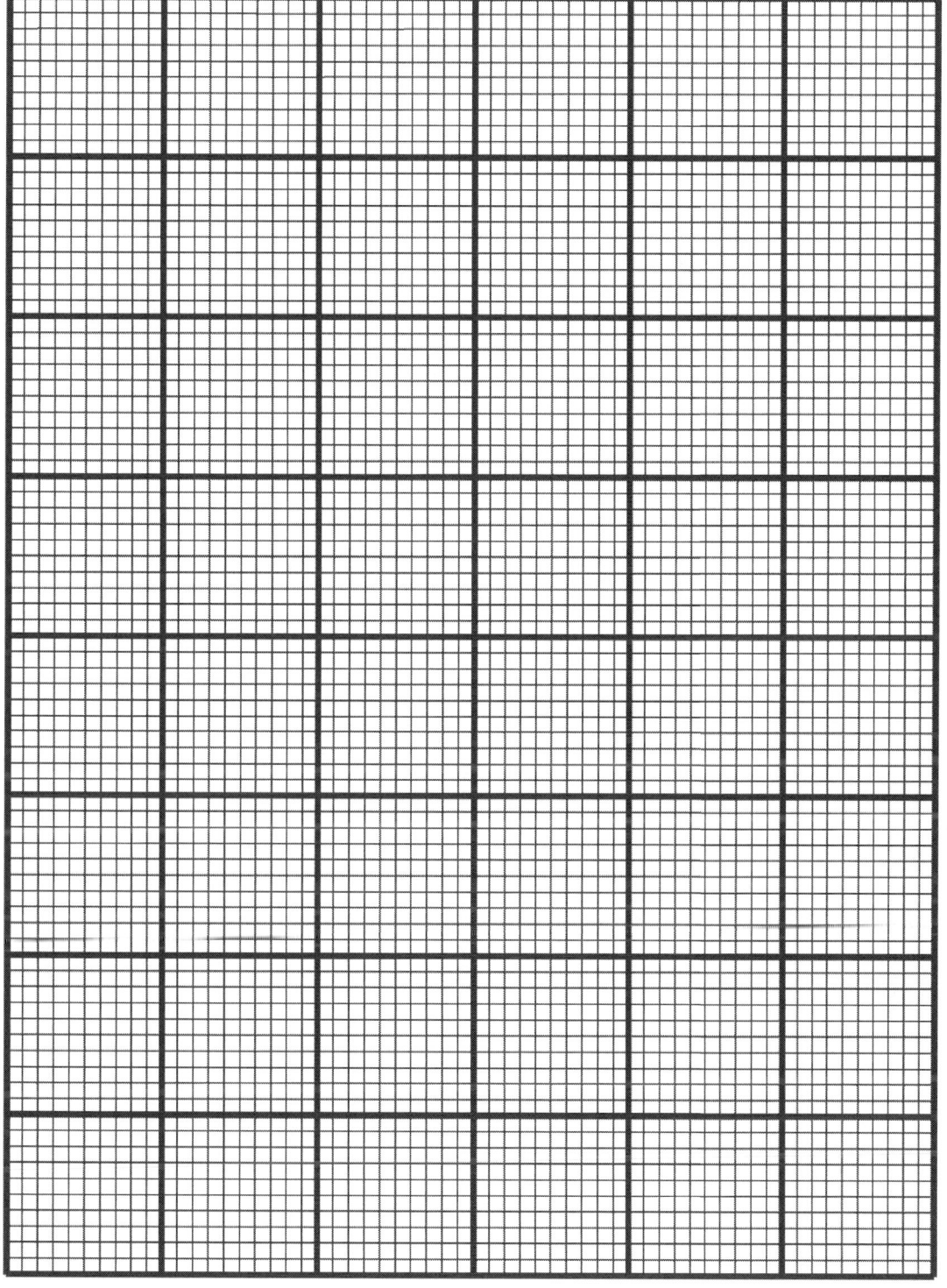

Floss Chart

	STRAND	TYPE	NUMBER	COLOR	ALTERNATE
•					
○					
■					
✚					
△					
◆					
=					
✖					
★					
⊙					
◳					
#					
▼					
☐					
☐					
▽					
→					
☽					

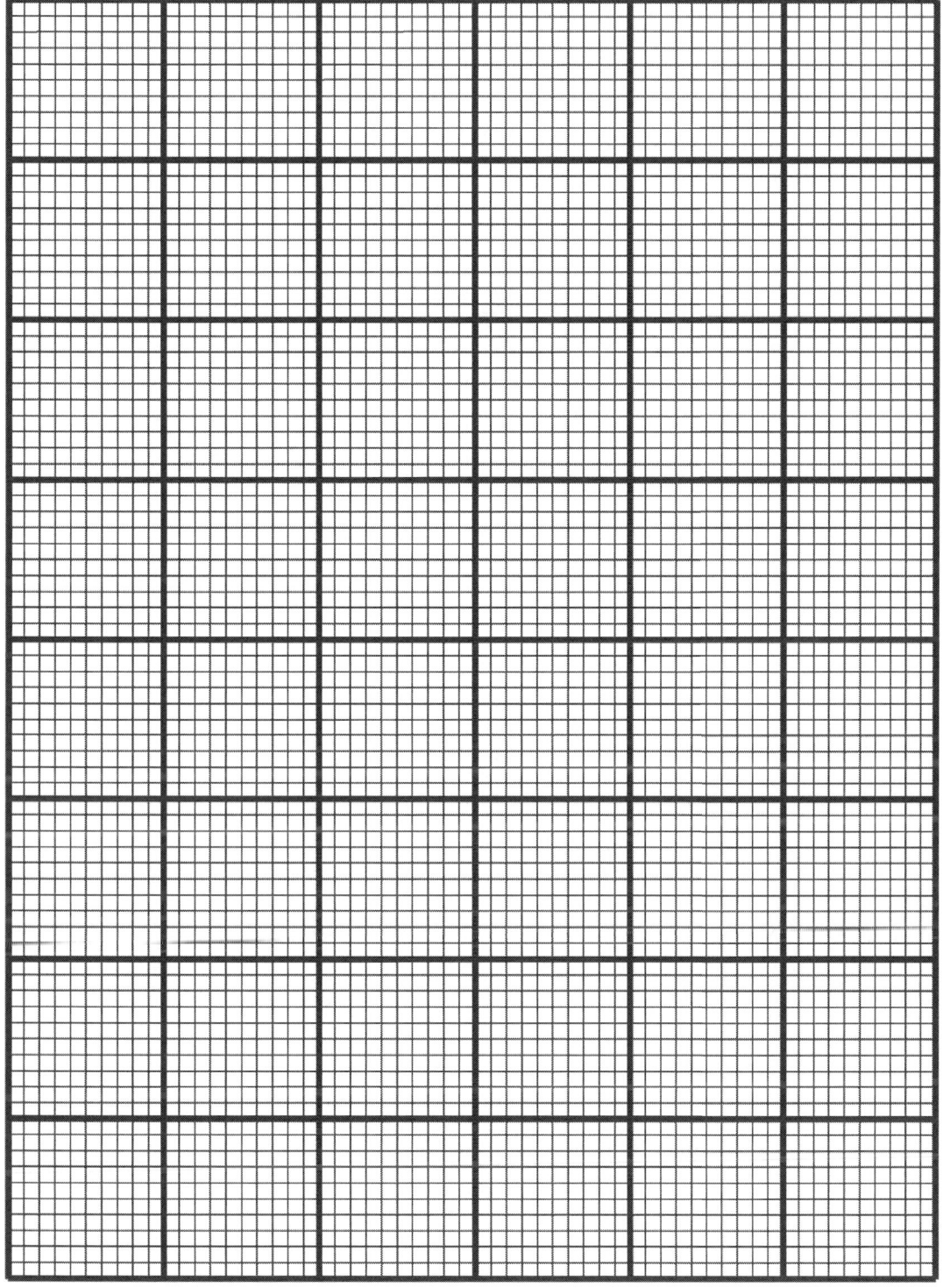

Floss Chart

	STRAND	TYPE	NUMBER	COLOR	ALTERNATE
•					
○					
■					
✚					
△					
◆					
=					
✖					
★					
⊙					
◳					
#					
▼					
☐					
☐					
▽					
→					
☽					

CROSS STITCH & NEEDLEPOINT CHART AND PATTERN SKETCHBOOK

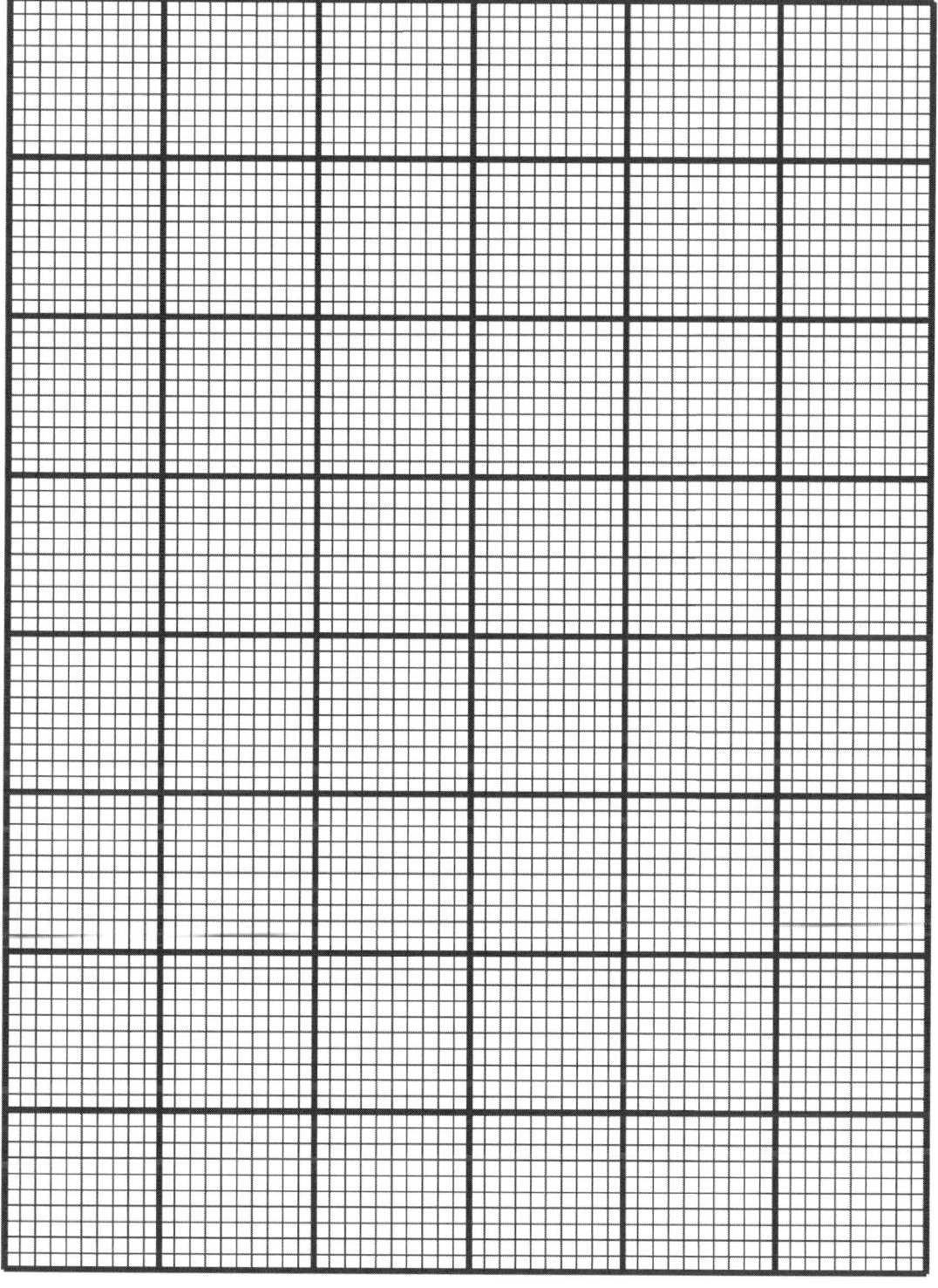

Floss Chart

	STRAND	TYPE	NUMBER	COLOR	ALTERNATE
•					
○					
■					
✚					
△					
◆					
=					
✖					
★					
⊙					
◘					
#					
▼					
☐					
☐					
▽					
→					
☽					

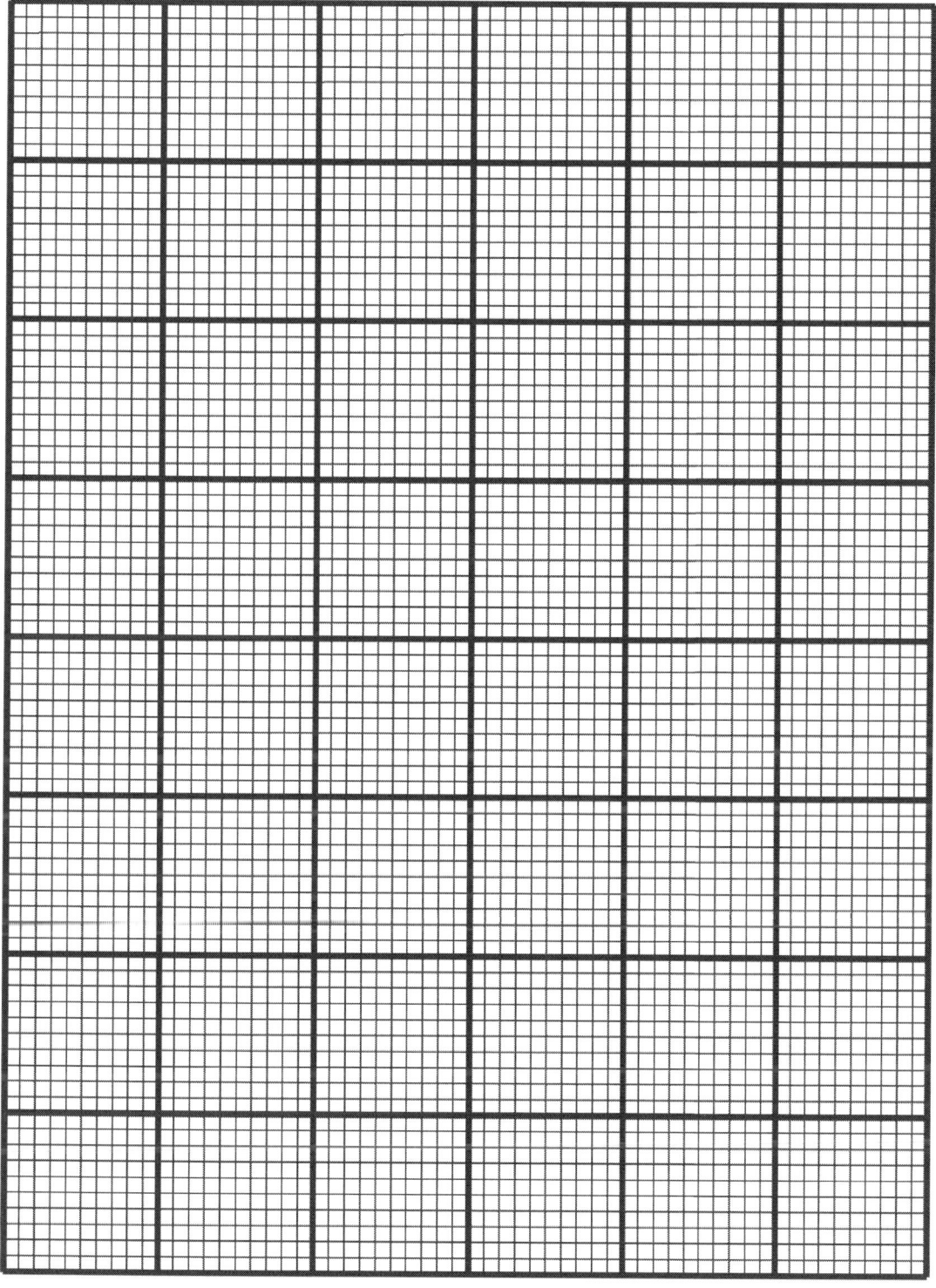

Floss Chart

	STRAND	TYPE	NUMBER	COLOR	ALTERNATE
•					
○					
■					
✚					
△					
◆					
=					
✖					
★					
⊙					
▫					
#					
▼					
☐					
☐					
▽					
→					
☾					

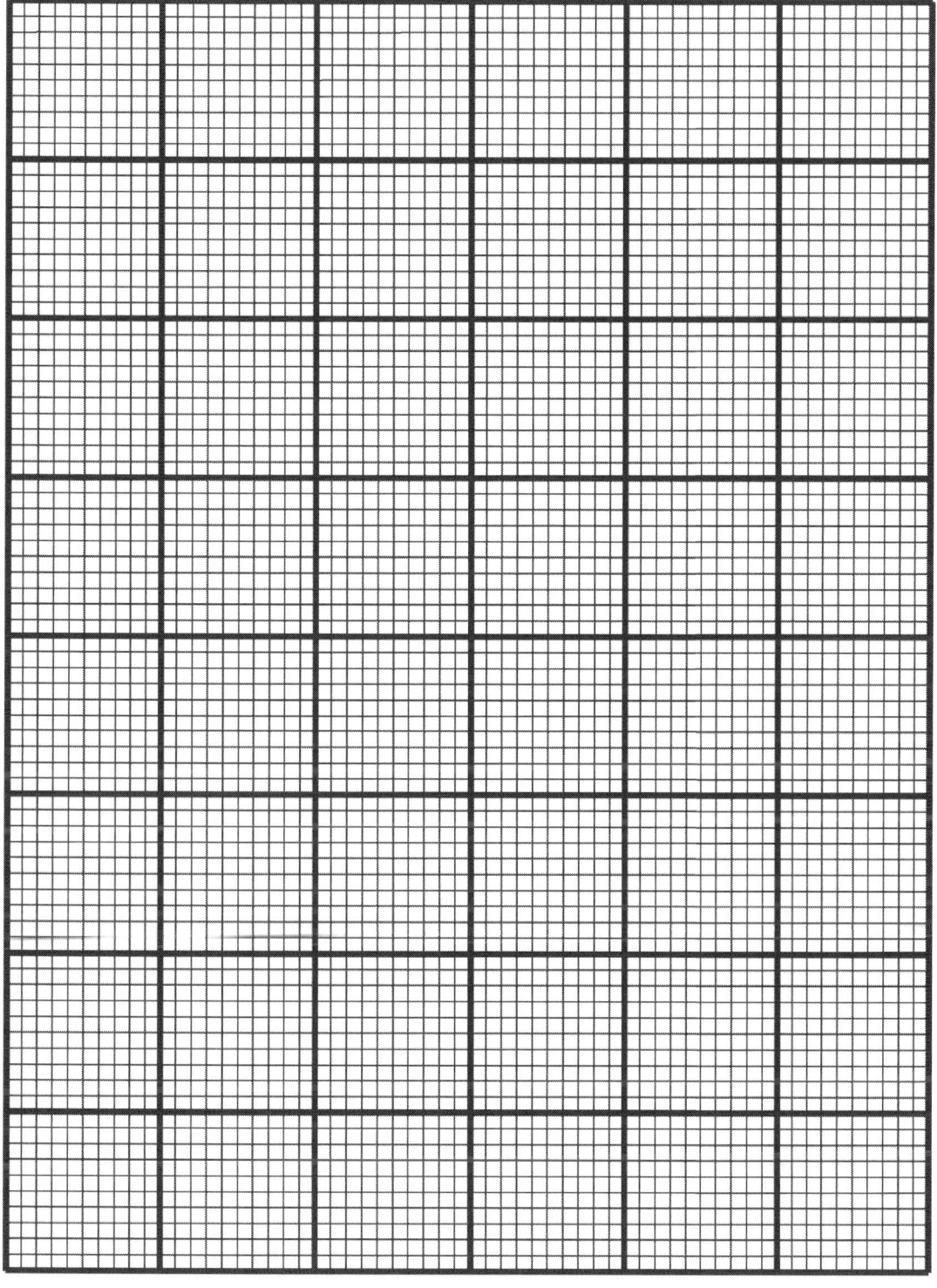

Floss Chart

	STRAND	TYPE	NUMBER	COLOR	ALTERNATE
•					
○					
■					
✚					
△					
◆					
=					
✖					
★					
⊙					
▫					
#					
▼					
□					
□					
▽					
→					
☾					

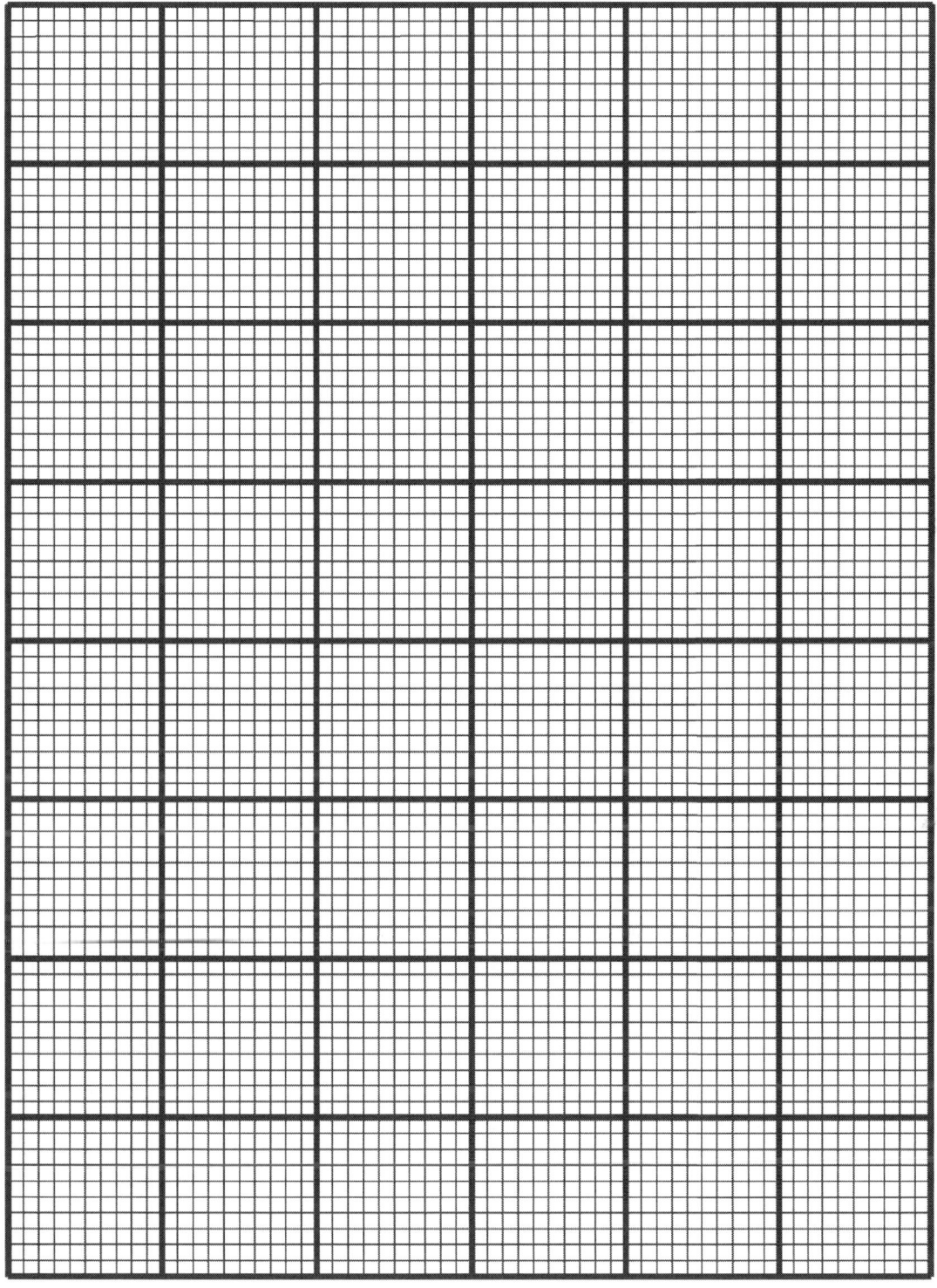

Floss Chart

	STRAND	TYPE	NUMBER	COLOR	ALTERNATE
•					
○					
■					
✚					
△					
◆					
=					
✖					
★					
⊙					
◱					
#					
▼					
☐					
☐					
▽					
→					
☽					

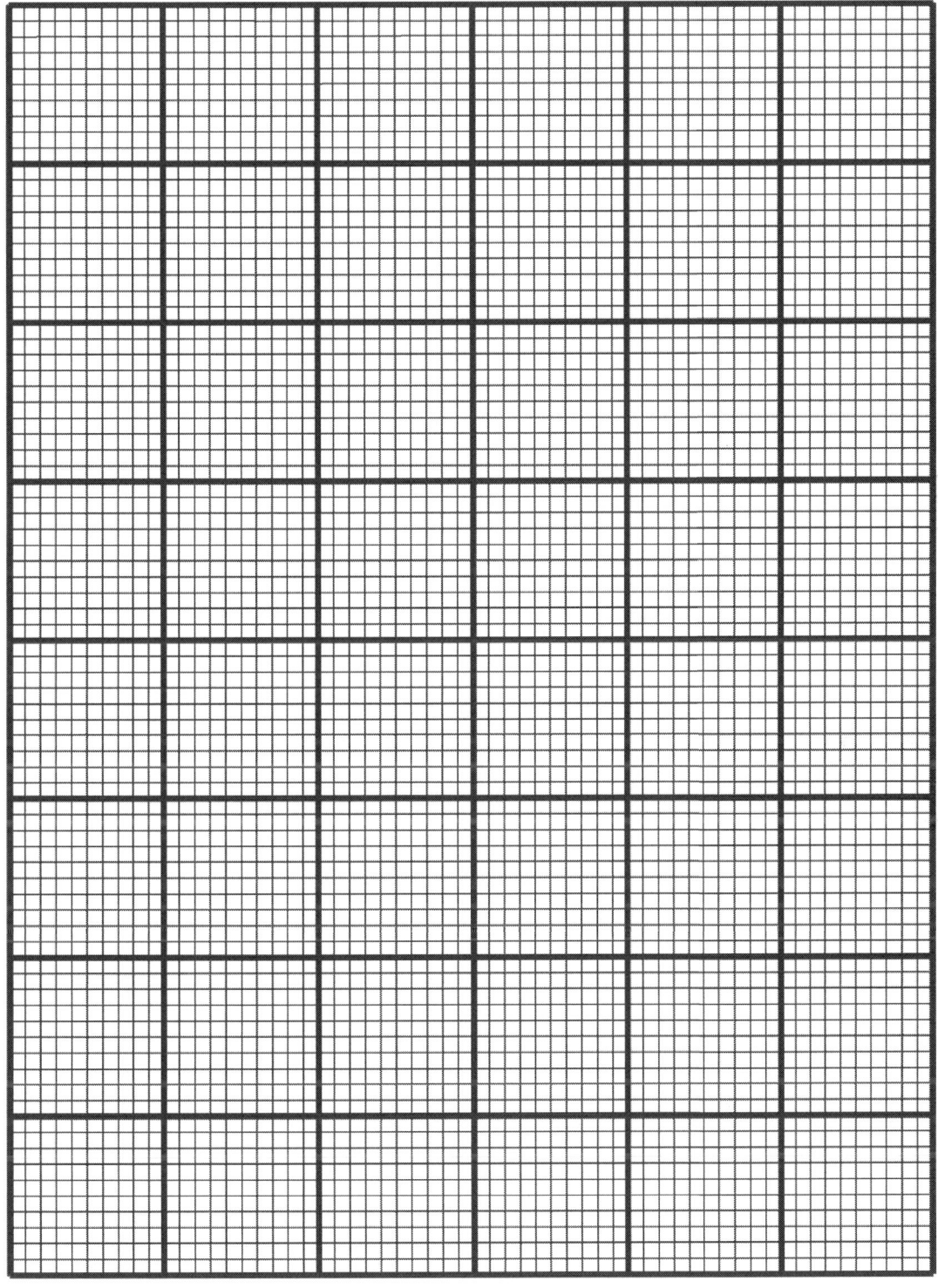

Floss Chart

	STRAND	TYPE	NUMBER	COLOR	ALTERNATE
•					
○					
■					
✛					
△					
◆					
=					
✖					
★					
⊙					
▫					
#					
▼					
□					
□					
▽					
→					
☽					

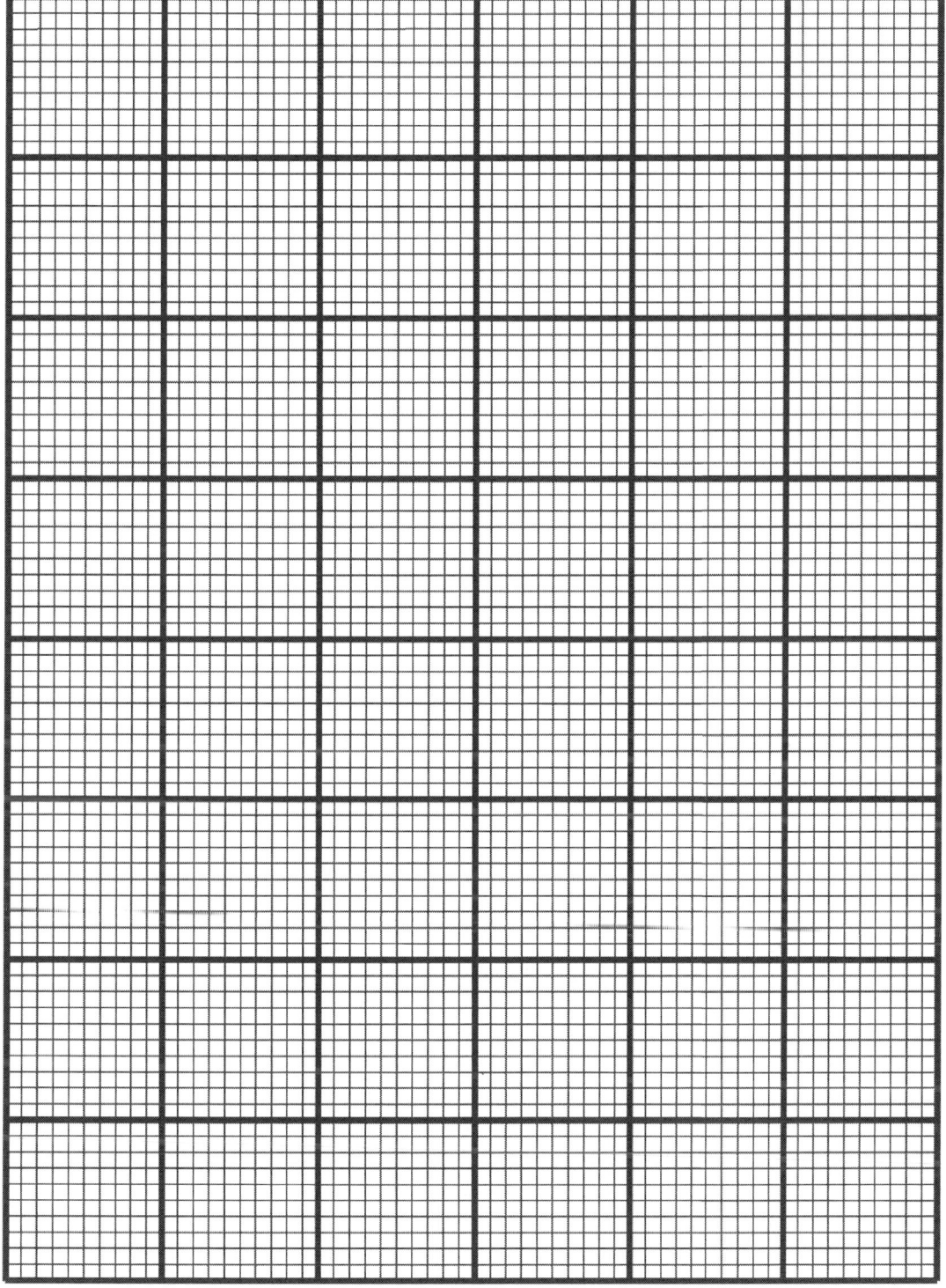

Floss Chart

	STRAND	TYPE	NUMBER	COLOR	ALTERNATE
•					
○					
■					
✚					
△					
◆					
=					
✖					
★					
⊙					
▫					
#					
▼					
☐					
☐					
▽					
→					
☾					

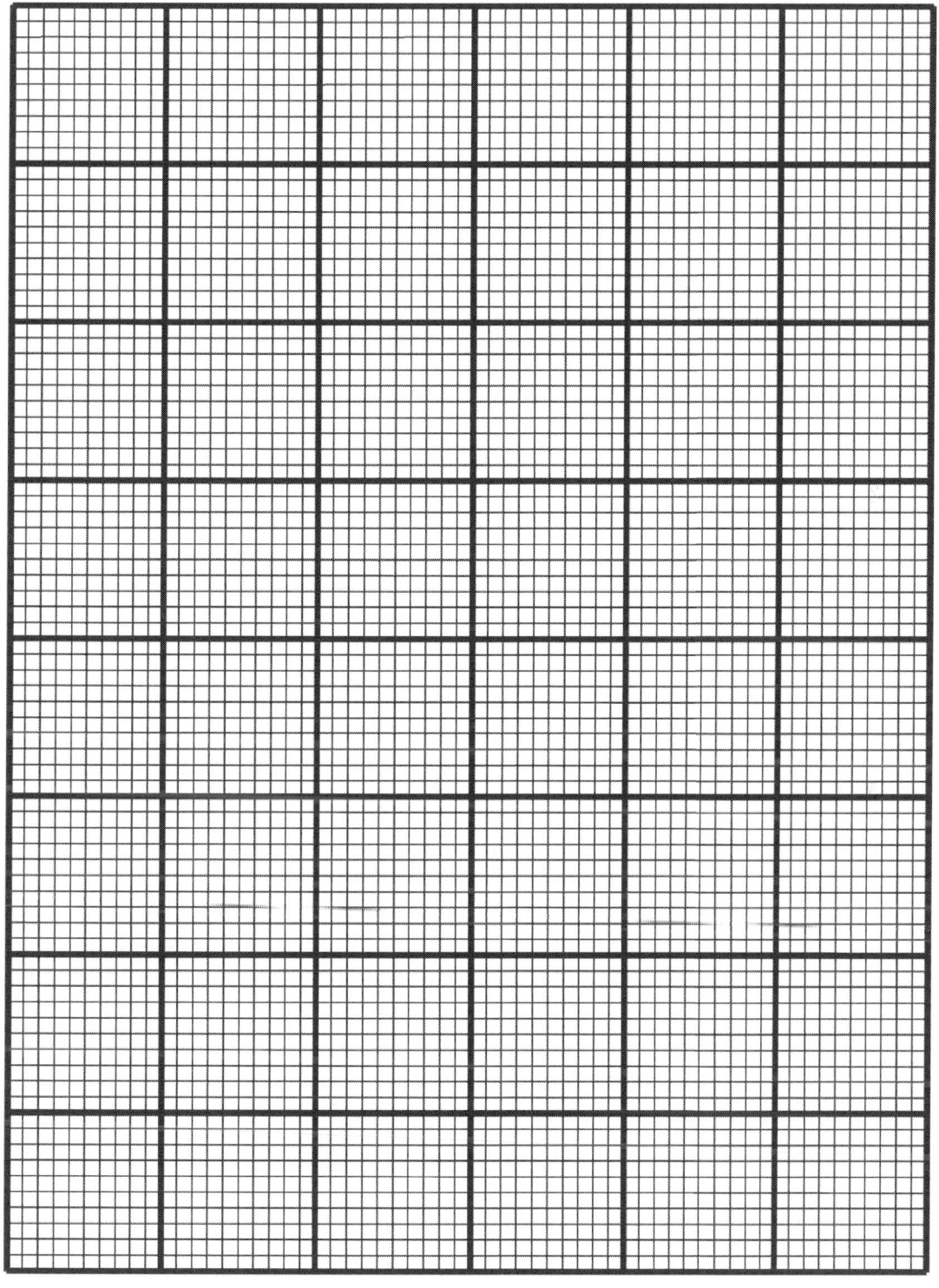

40 X 60 Stitch Count

10-Square Graph Grids

Floss Chart

	STRAND	TYPE	NUMBER	COLOR	ALTERNATE
●					
○					
■					
✚					
△					
◆					
=					
✖					
★					
⊙					
▣					
#					
▼					
☐					
☐					
▽					
→					
☽					

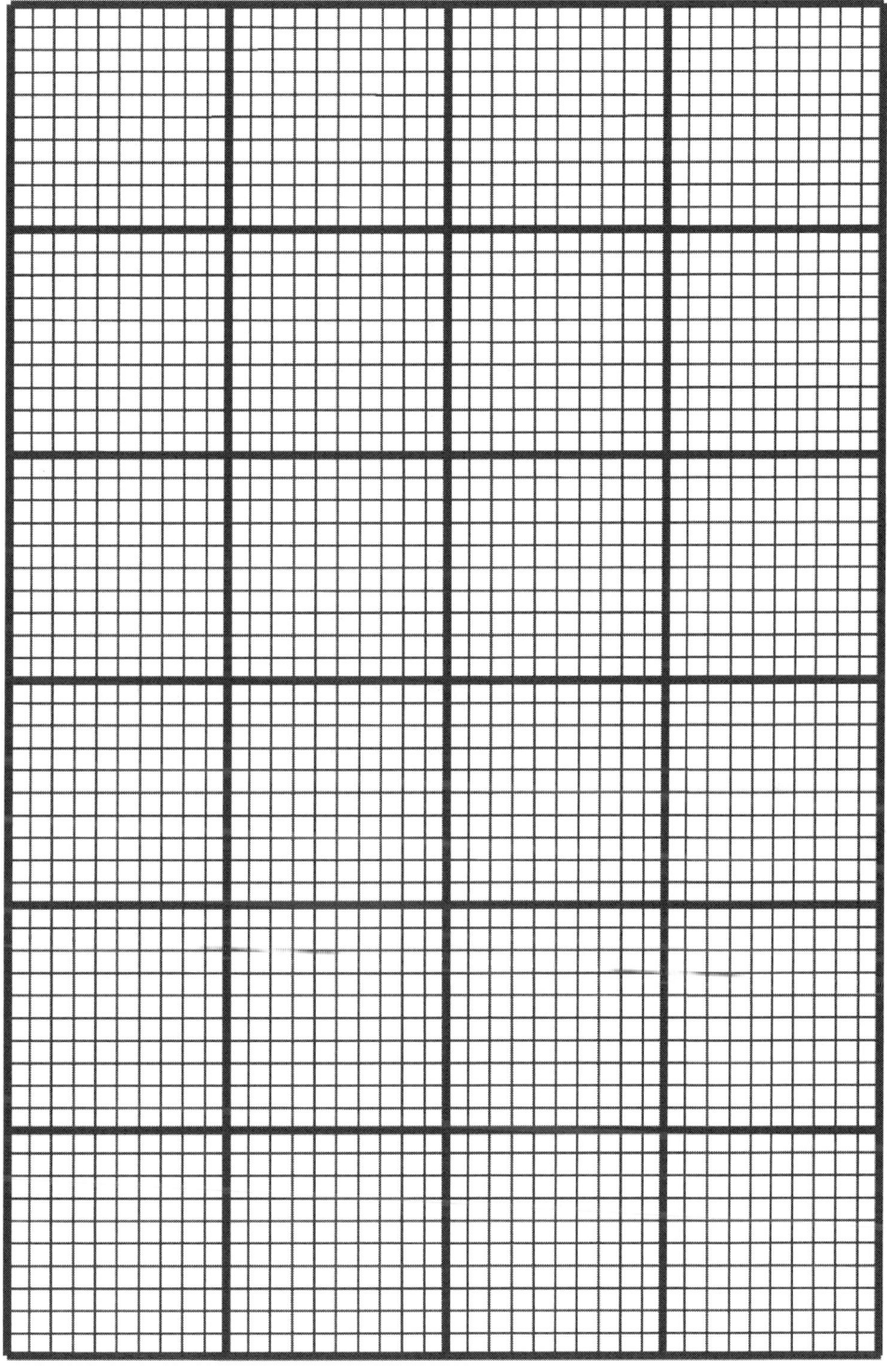

Floss Chart

	STRAND	TYPE	NUMBER	COLOR	ALTERNATE
•					
○					
■					
✚					
△					
◆					
=					
✖					
★					
⊙					
▫					
#					
▼					
☐					
☐					
▽					
→					
☽					

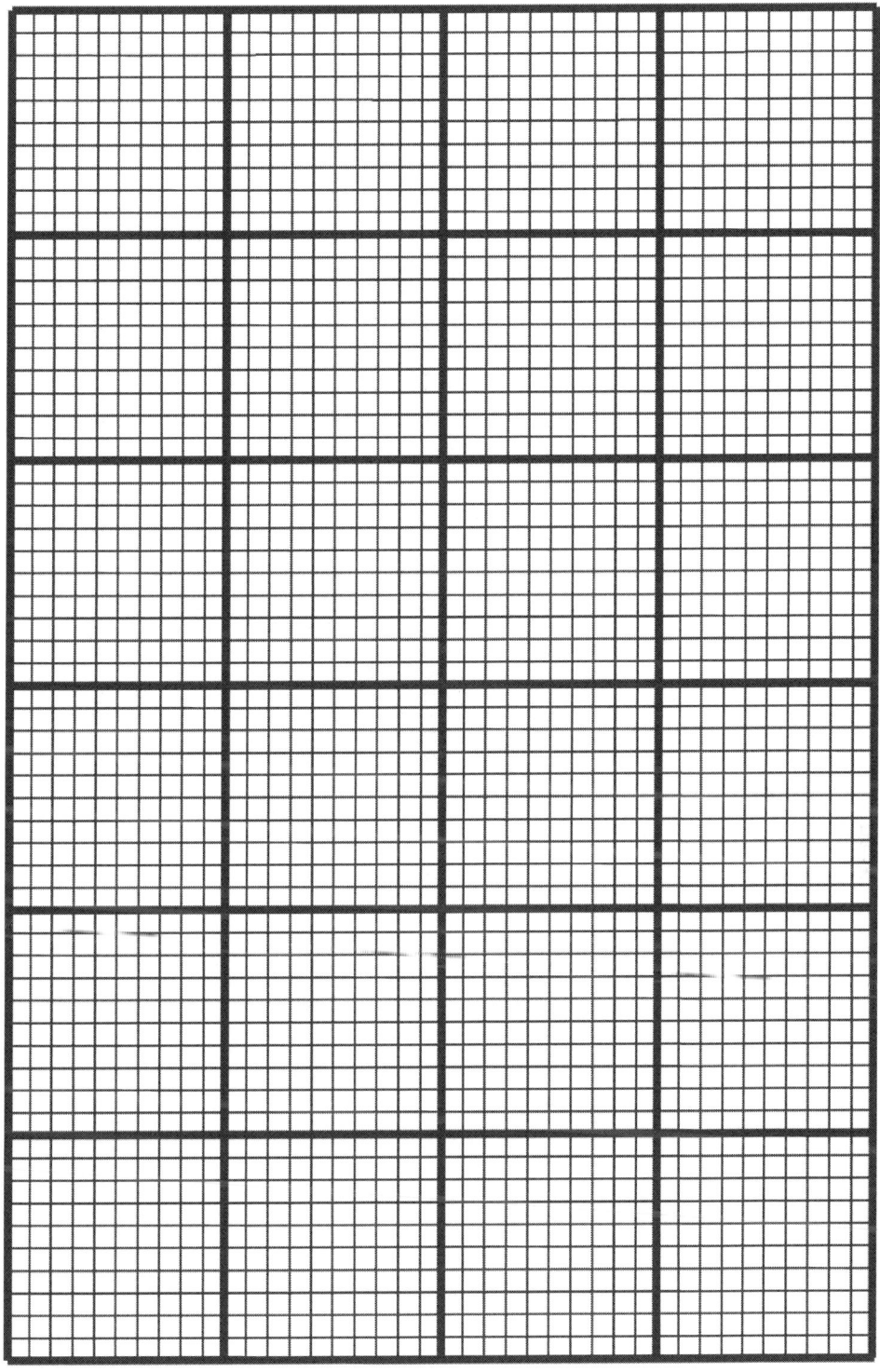

Floss Chart

	STRAND	TYPE	NUMBER	COLOR	ALTERNATE
•					
○					
■					
✚					
△					
◆					
=					
✖					
★					
⊙					
◘					
#					
▼					
☐					
☐					
▽					
→					
☾					

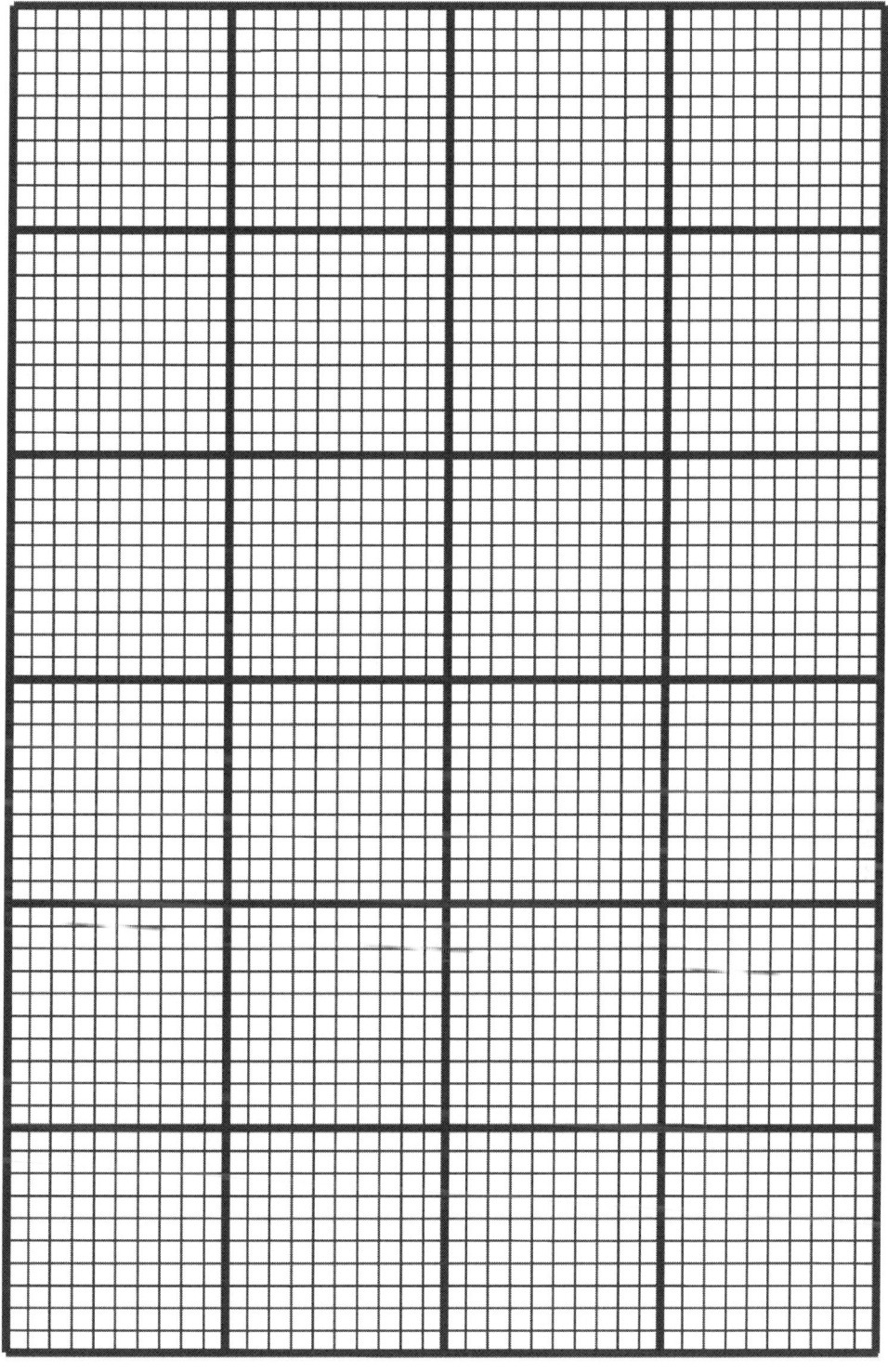

Floss Chart

	STRAND	TYPE	NUMBER	COLOR	ALTERNATE
●					
○					
■					
✚					
△					
◆					
=					
✖					
★					
⊙					
▣					
#					
▼					
▢					
▢					
▽					
→					
☽					

CROSS STITCH & NEEDLEPOINT CHART AND PATTERN SKETCHBOOK

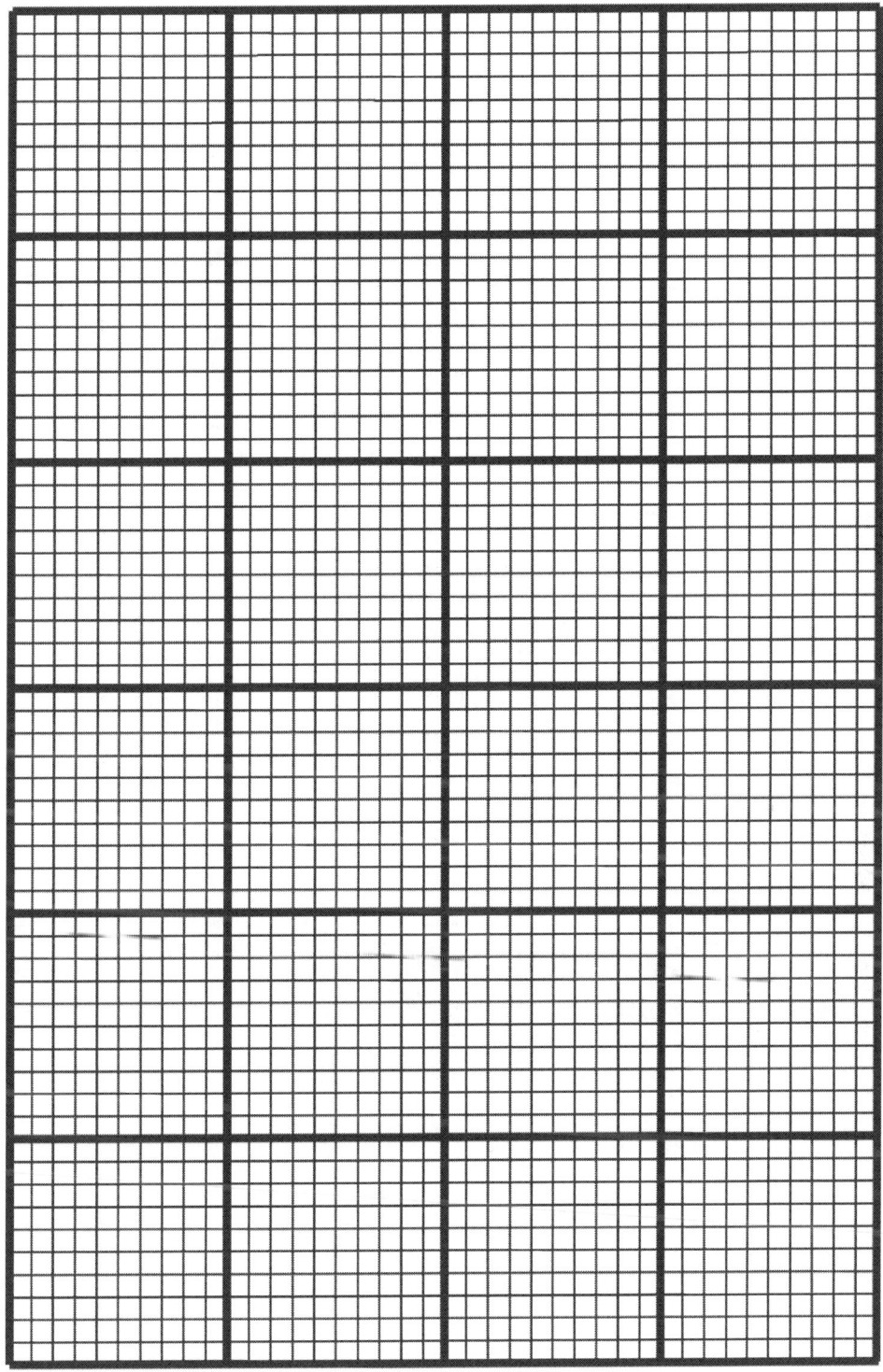

Floss Chart

	STRAND	TYPE	NUMBER	COLOR	ALTERNATE
•					
○					
■					
✚					
△					
◆					
=					
✖					
★					
⊙					
▫					
#					
▼					
☐					
☐					
▽					
→					
☾					

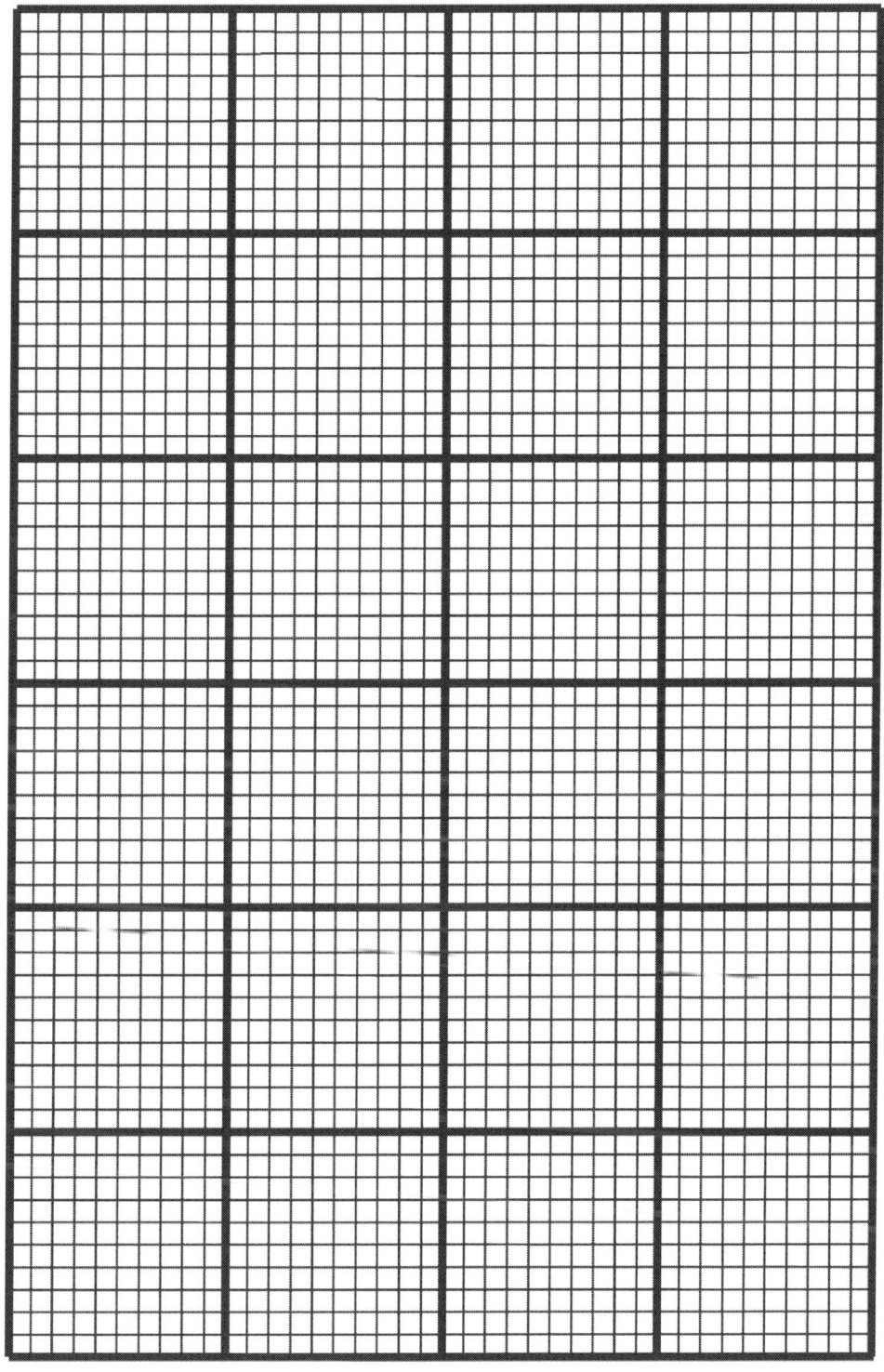

Hoop & Thread Needlework Design

Floss Chart

	STRAND	TYPE	NUMBER	COLOR	ALTERNATE
•					
○					
■					
✚					
△					
◆					
=					
✖					
★					
⊙					
▫					
#					
▼					
☐					
☐					
▽					
→					
☽					

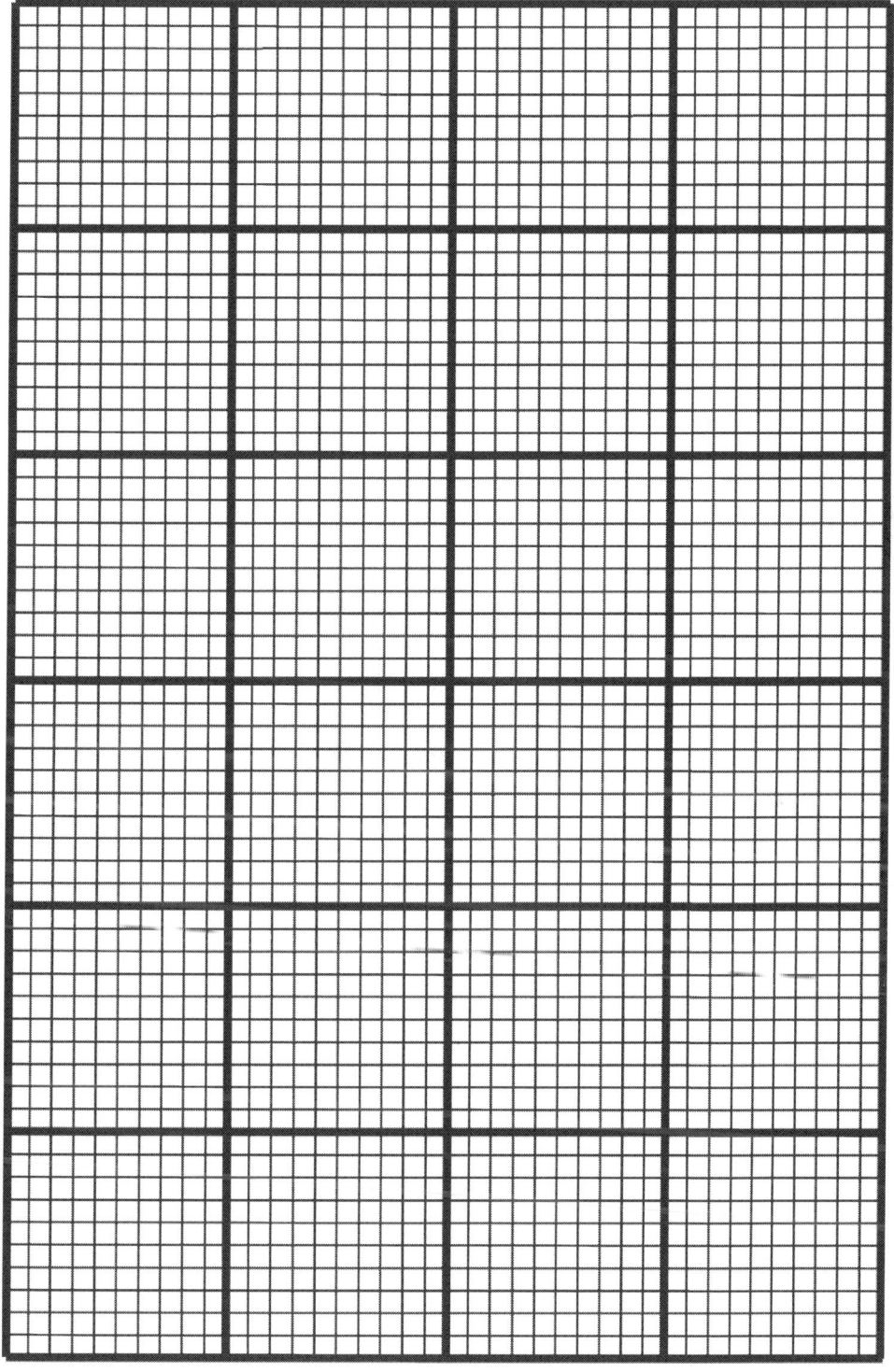

Floss Chart

	STRAND	TYPE	NUMBER	COLOR	ALTERNATE
•					
○					
■					
✚					
△					
◆					
=					
✖					
★					
⊙					
▫					
#					
▼					
□					
□					
▽					
→					
☽					

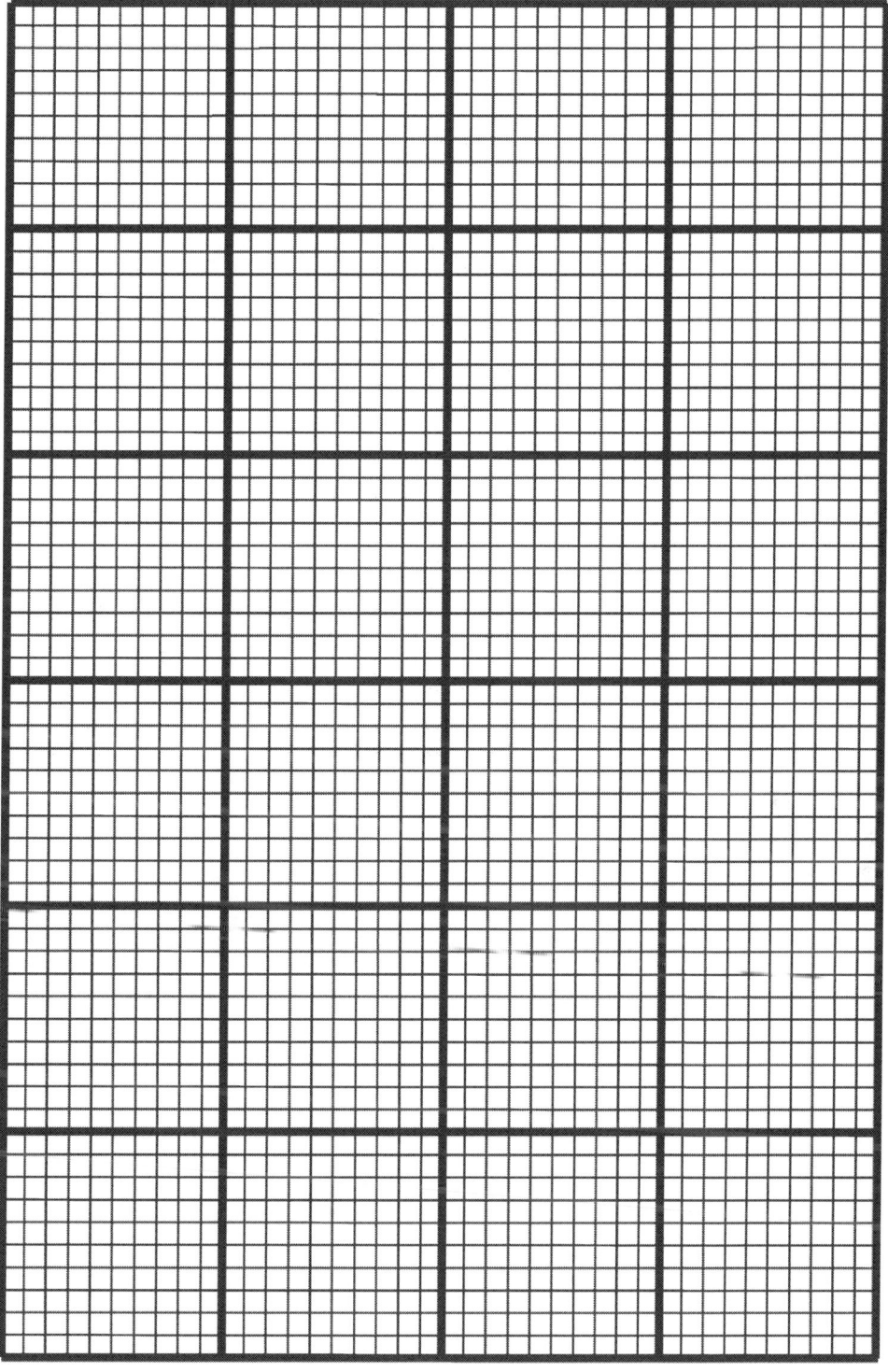

Floss Chart

	STRAND	TYPE	NUMBER	COLOR	ALTERNATE
•					
○					
■					
✚					
△					
◆					
=					
✖					
★					
⊙					
▣					
#					
▼					
☐					
☐					
▽					
→					
☾					

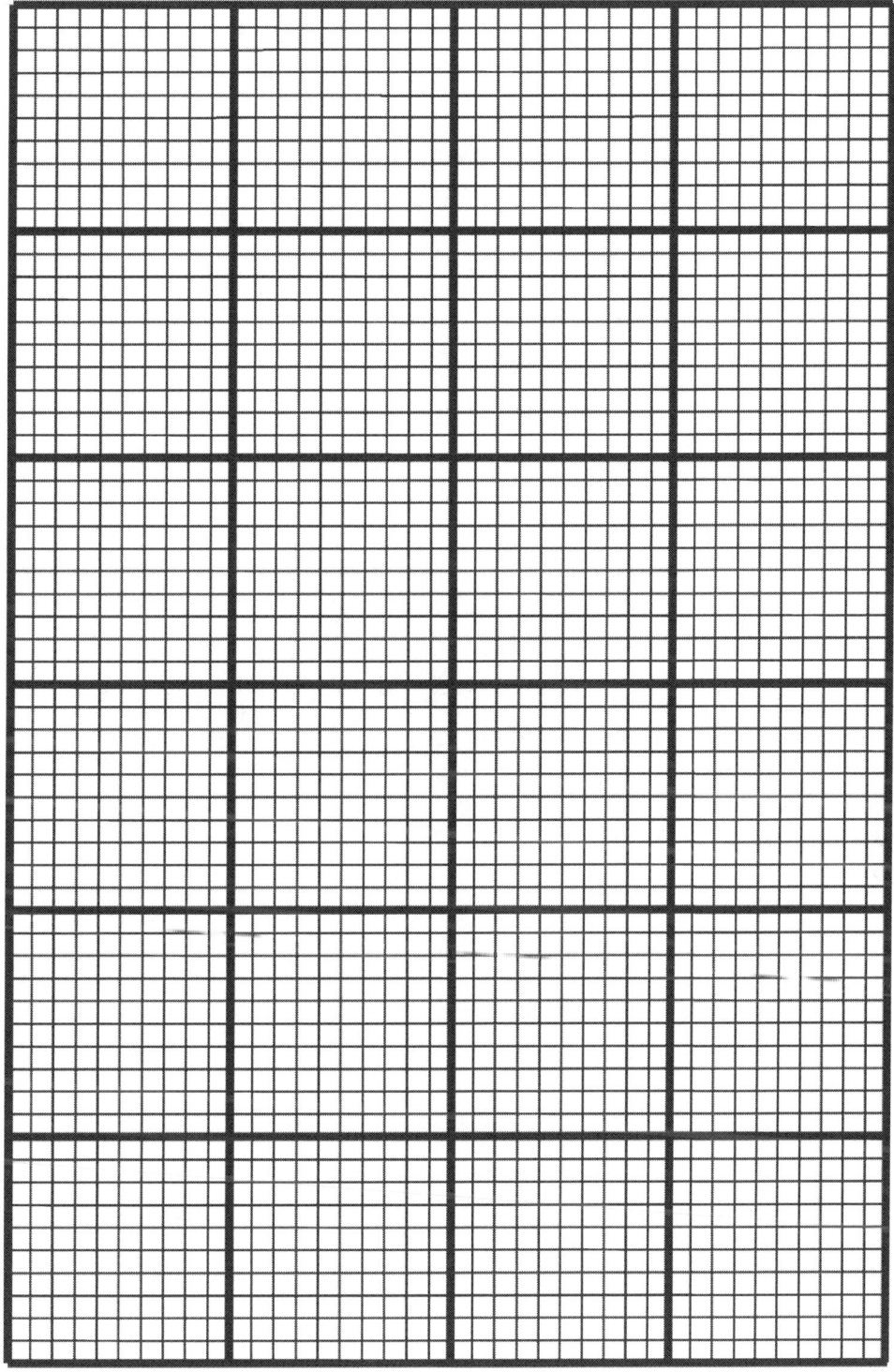

Floss Chart

	STRAND	TYPE	NUMBER	COLOR	ALTERNATE
•					
○					
■					
✚					
△					
◆					
=					
✖					
★					
⊙					
◘					
#					
▼					
☐					
☐					
▽					
→					
☽					

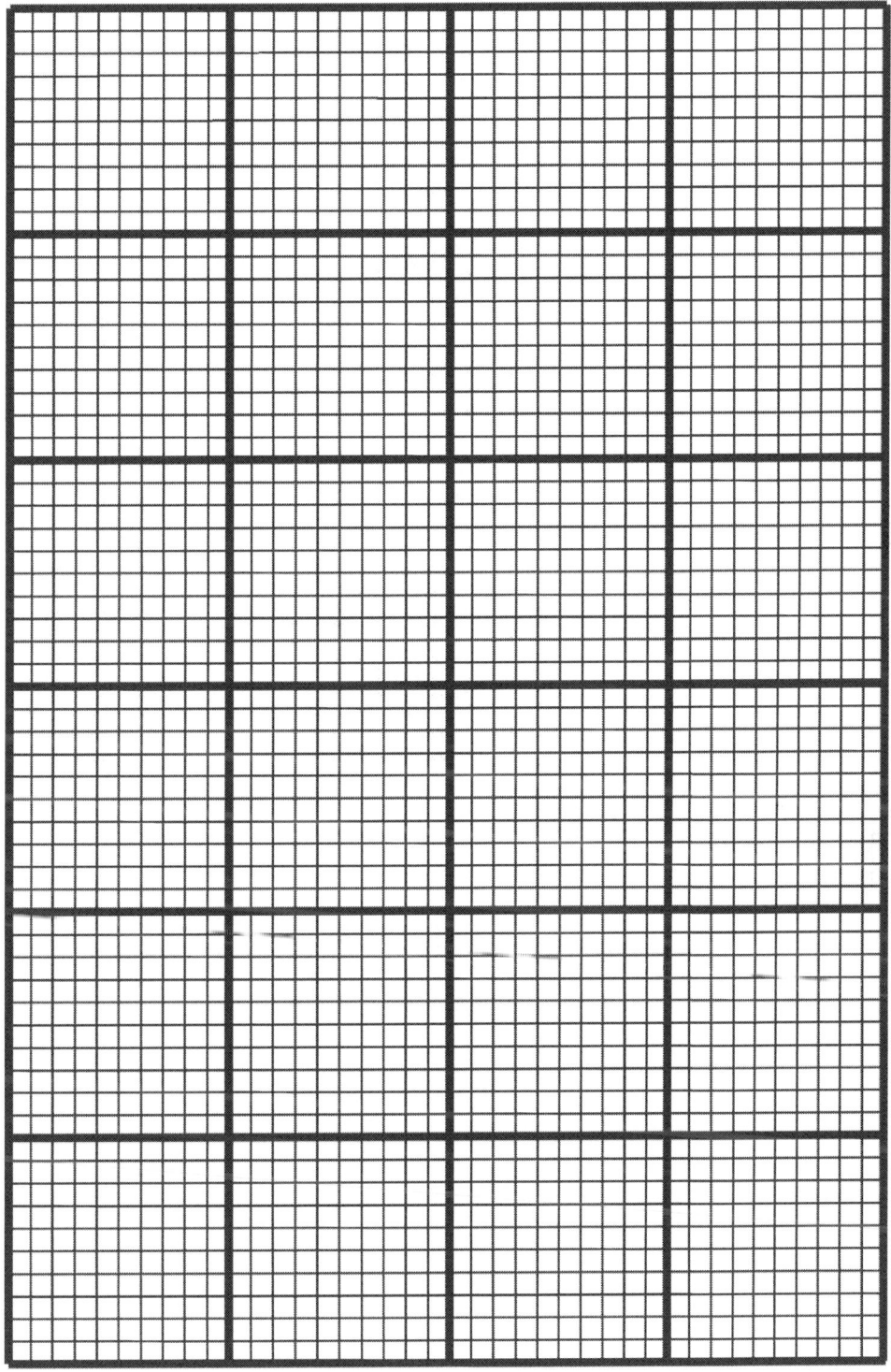

Floss Chart

	STRAND	TYPE	NUMBER	COLOR	ALTERNATE
•					
○					
■					
✚					
△					
◆					
=					
✖					
★					
⊙					
▣					
#					
▼					
□					
□					
▽					
→					
☽					

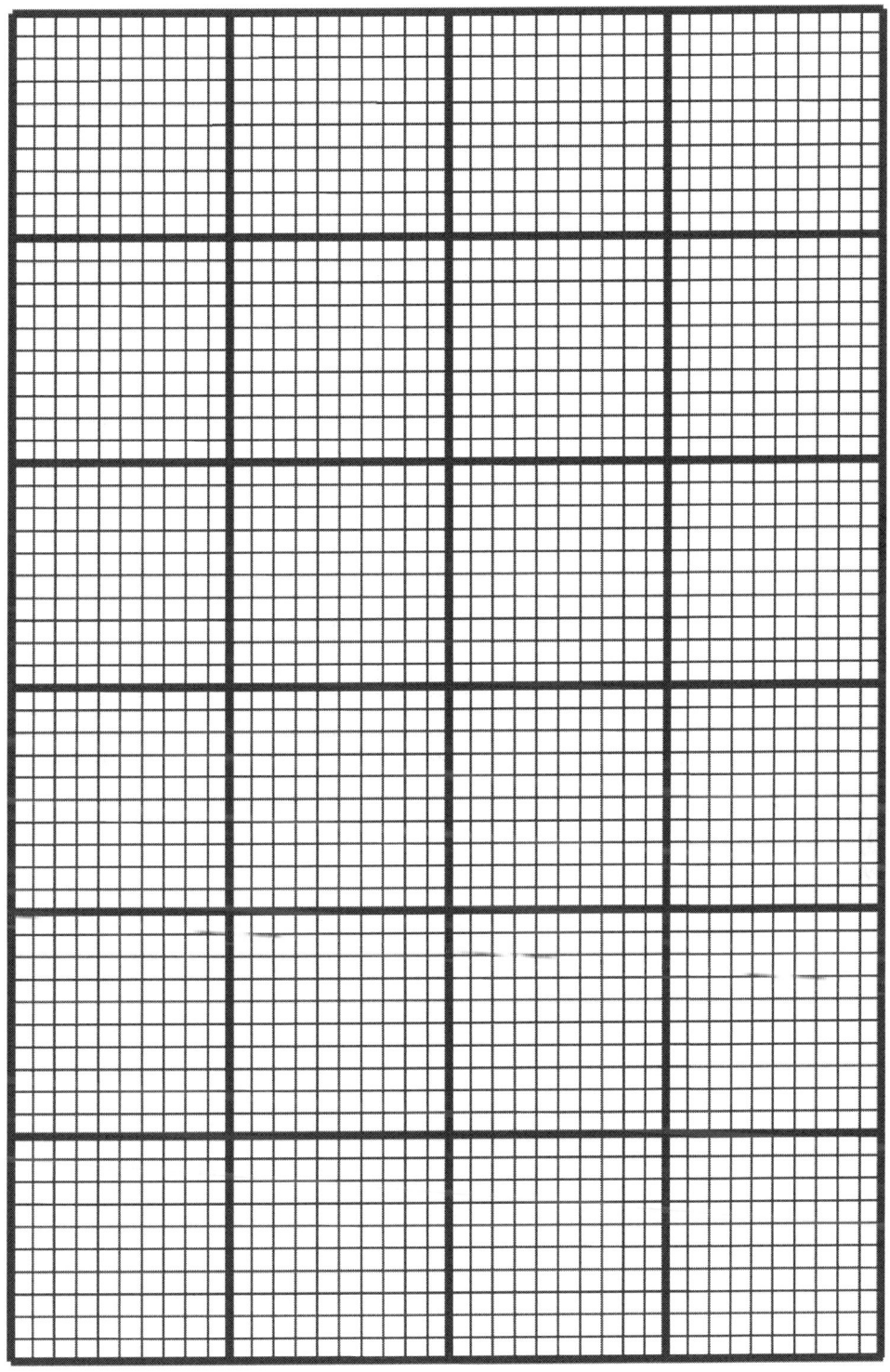

Floss Chart

	STRAND	TYPE	NUMBER	COLOR	ALTERNATE
•					
○					
■					
✚					
△					
◆					
=					
✖					
★					
⊙					
▢					
#					
▼					
☐					
☐					
▽					
→					
☾					

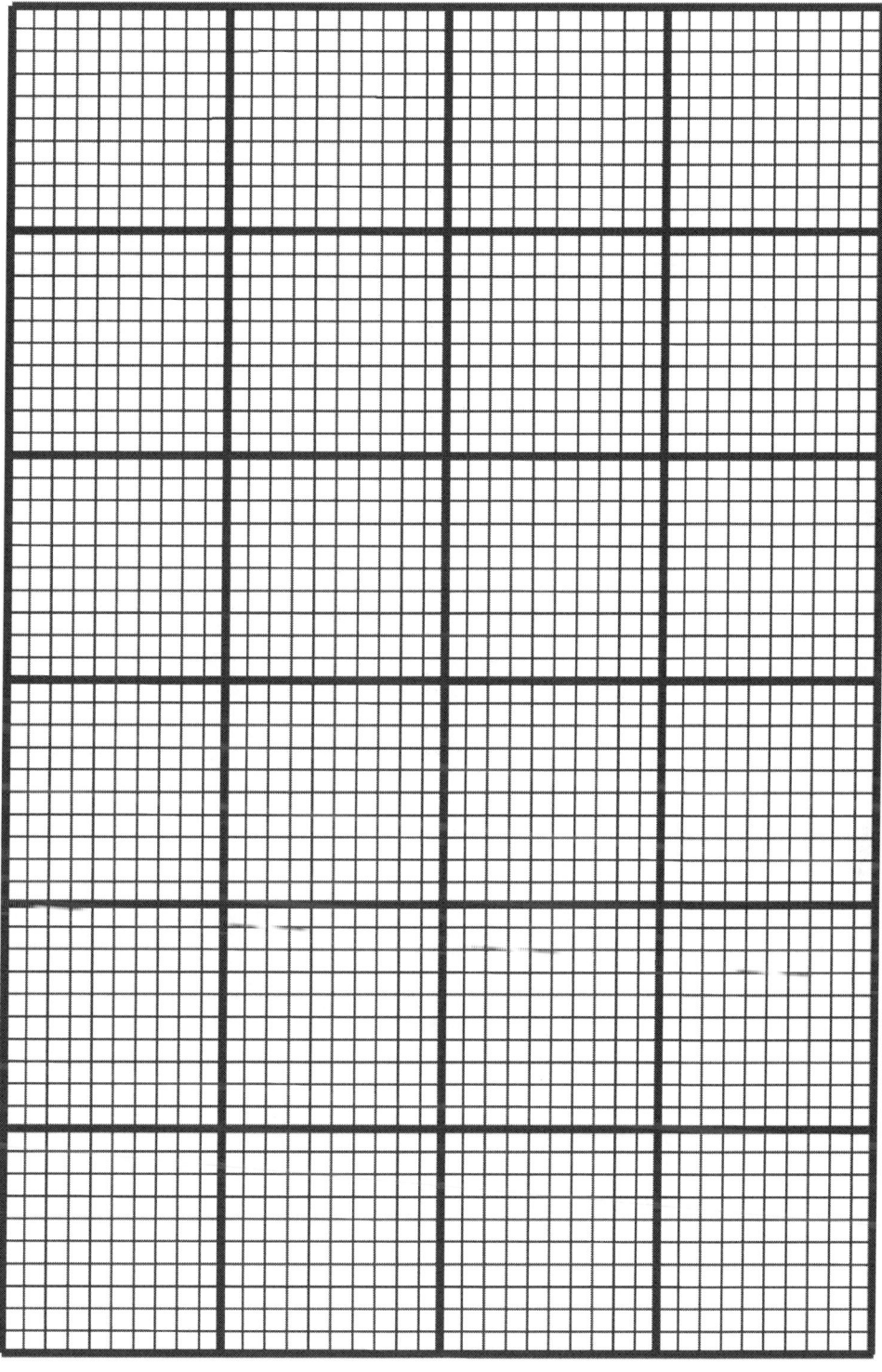

Floss Chart

	STRAND	TYPE	NUMBER	COLOR	ALTERNATE
•					
○					
■					
✚					
△					
◆					
=					
✖					
★					
⊙					
▣					
#					
▼					
□					
□					
▽					
→					
☾					

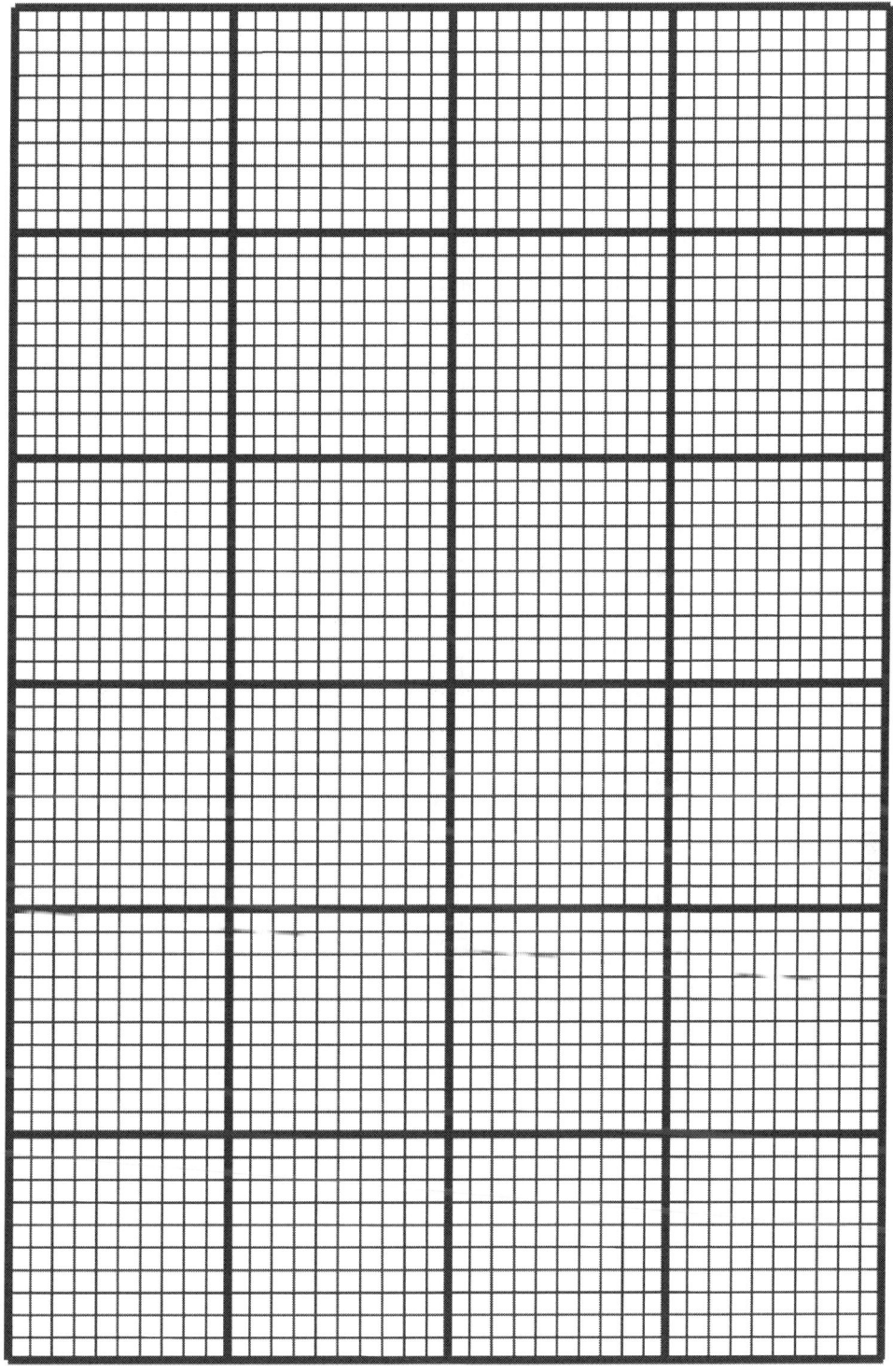

Floss Chart

Symbol	STRAND	TYPE	NUMBER	COLOR	ALTERNATE
•					
○					
■					
✚					
△					
◆					
=					
✖					
★					
⊙					
▫					
#					
▼					
□					
□					
▽					
→					
☽					

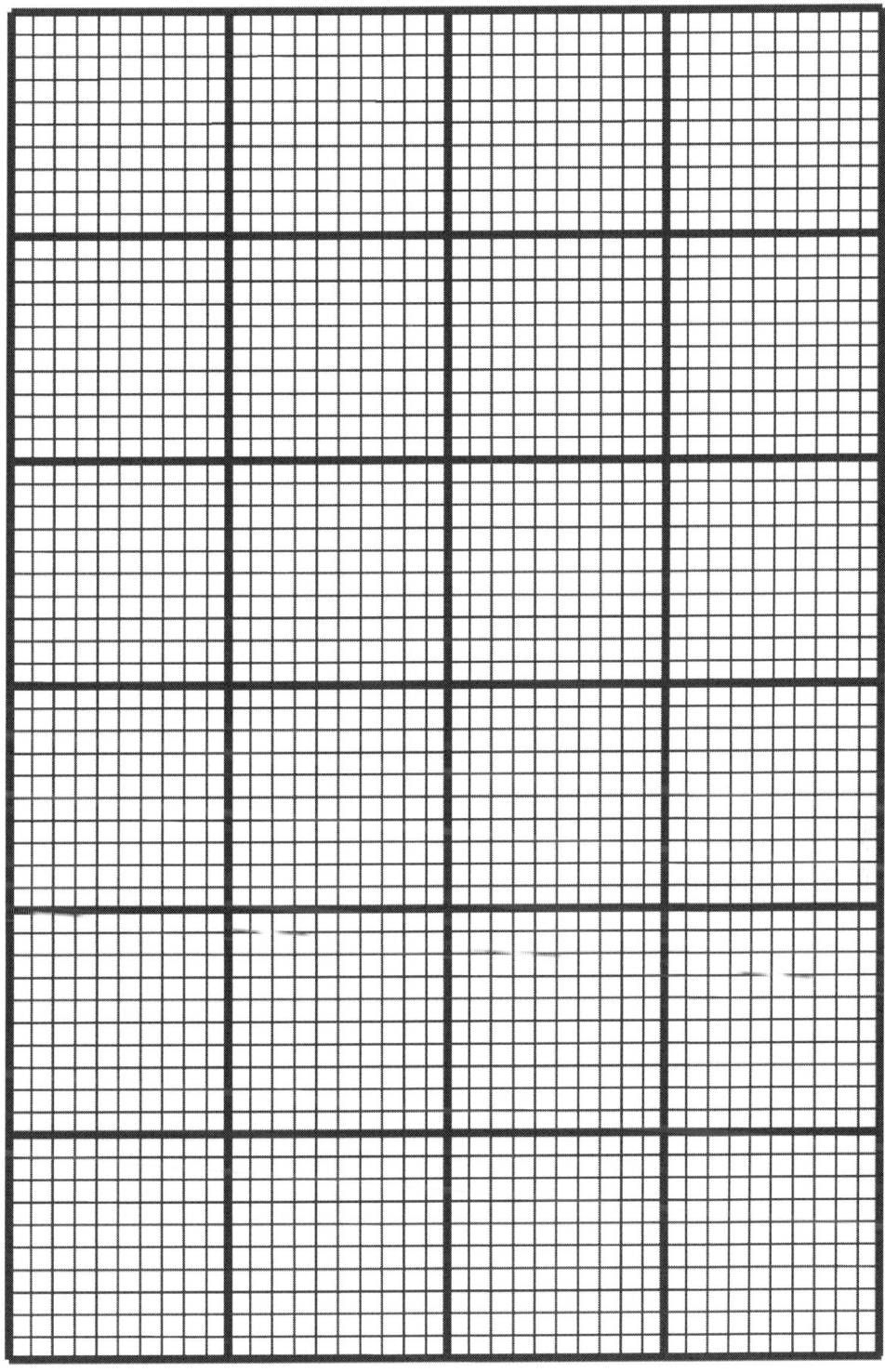

Floss Chart

	STRAND	TYPE	NUMBER	COLOR	ALTERNATE
●					
○					
■					
✚					
△					
◆					
=					
✖					
★					
⊙					
▫					
#					
▼					
☐					
☐					
▽					
→					
☾					

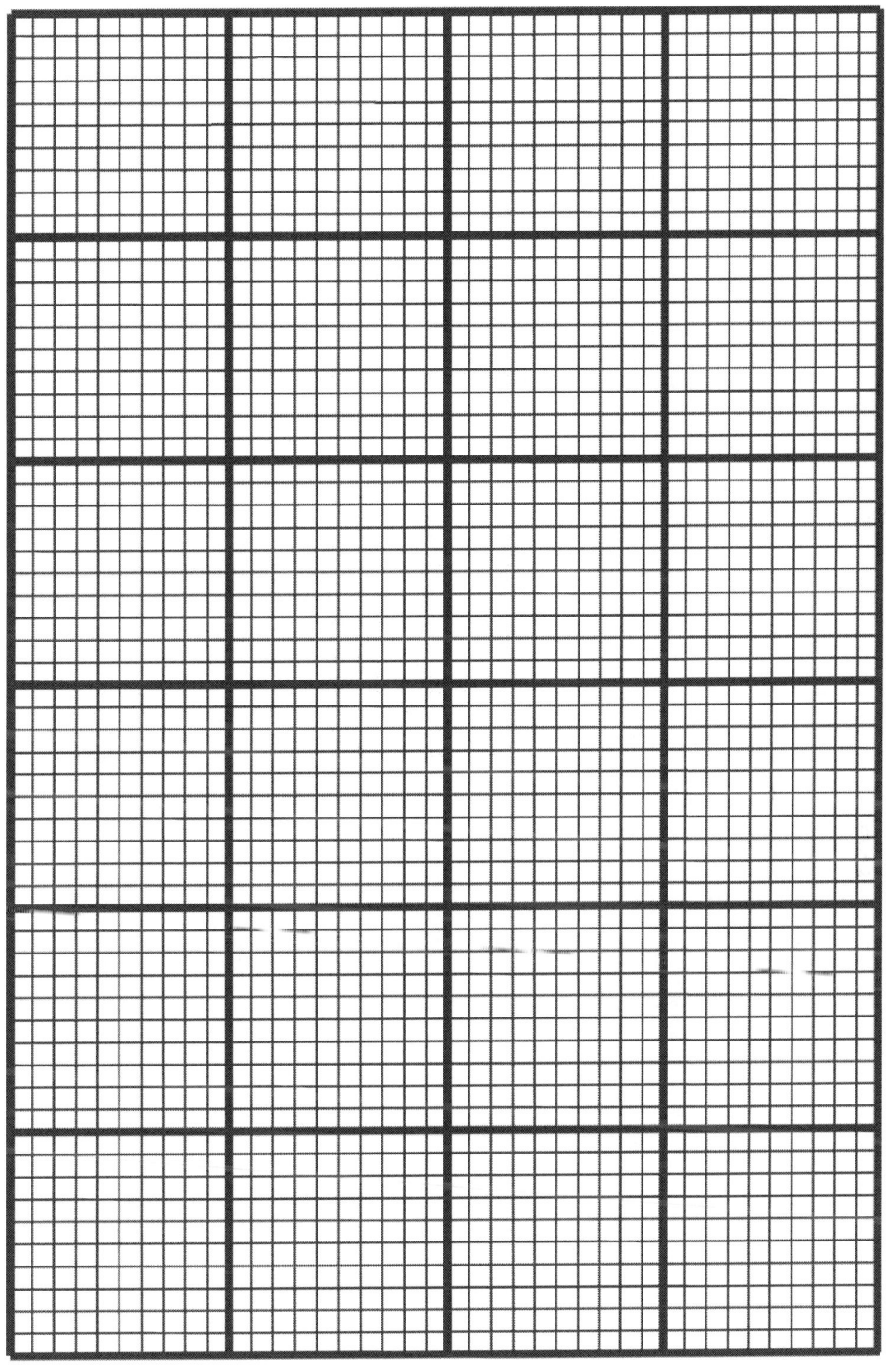

Floss Chart

	STRAND	TYPE	NUMBER	COLOR	ALTERNATE
•					
○					
■					
✚					
△					
◆					
=					
✖					
★					
⊙					
◻					
#					
▼					
□					
□					
▽					
→					
☾					

CROSS STITCH & NEEDLEPOINT CHART AND PATTERN SKETCHBOOK

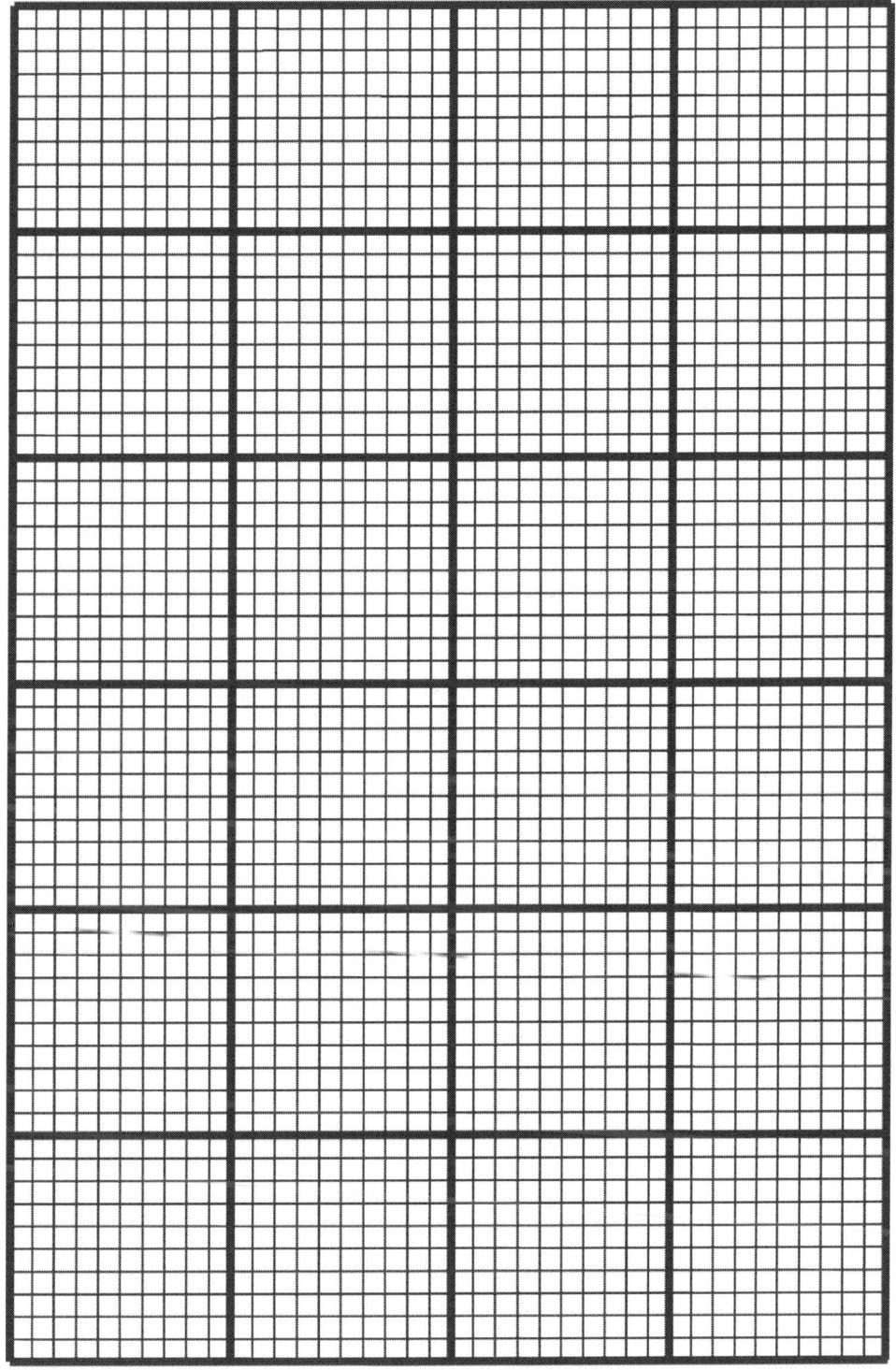

Floss Chart

	STRAND	TYPE	NUMBER	COLOR	ALTERNATE
•					
○					
■					
✚					
△					
◆					
=					
✖					
★					
⊙					
◘					
#					
▼					
☐					
☐					
▽					
→					
☽					

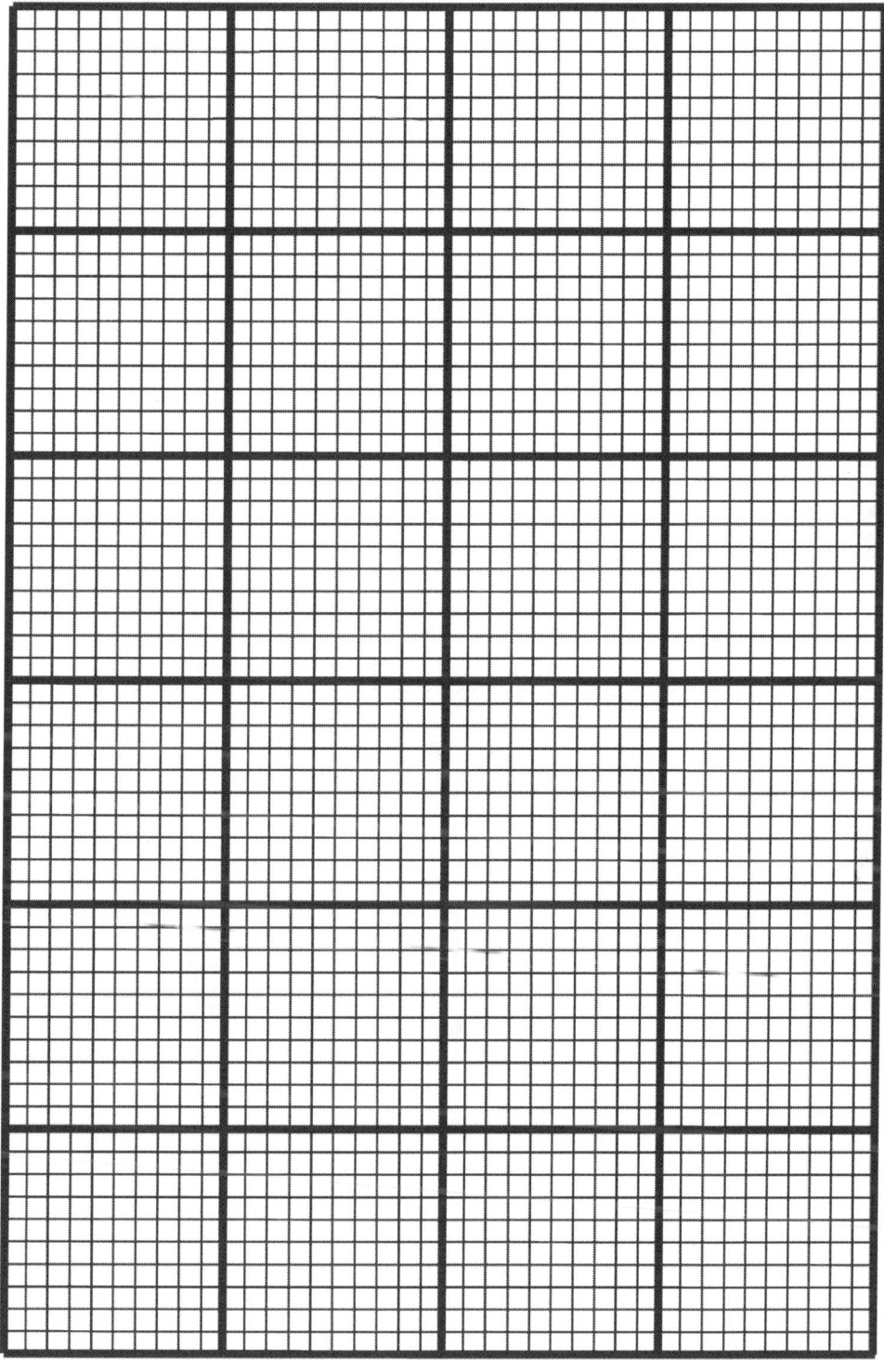

Floss Chart

	STRAND	TYPE	NUMBER	COLOR	ALTERNATE
•					
○					
■					
✚					
△					
◆					
=					
✖					
★					
⊙					
◲					
#					
▼					
☐					
☐					
▽					
→					
☽					

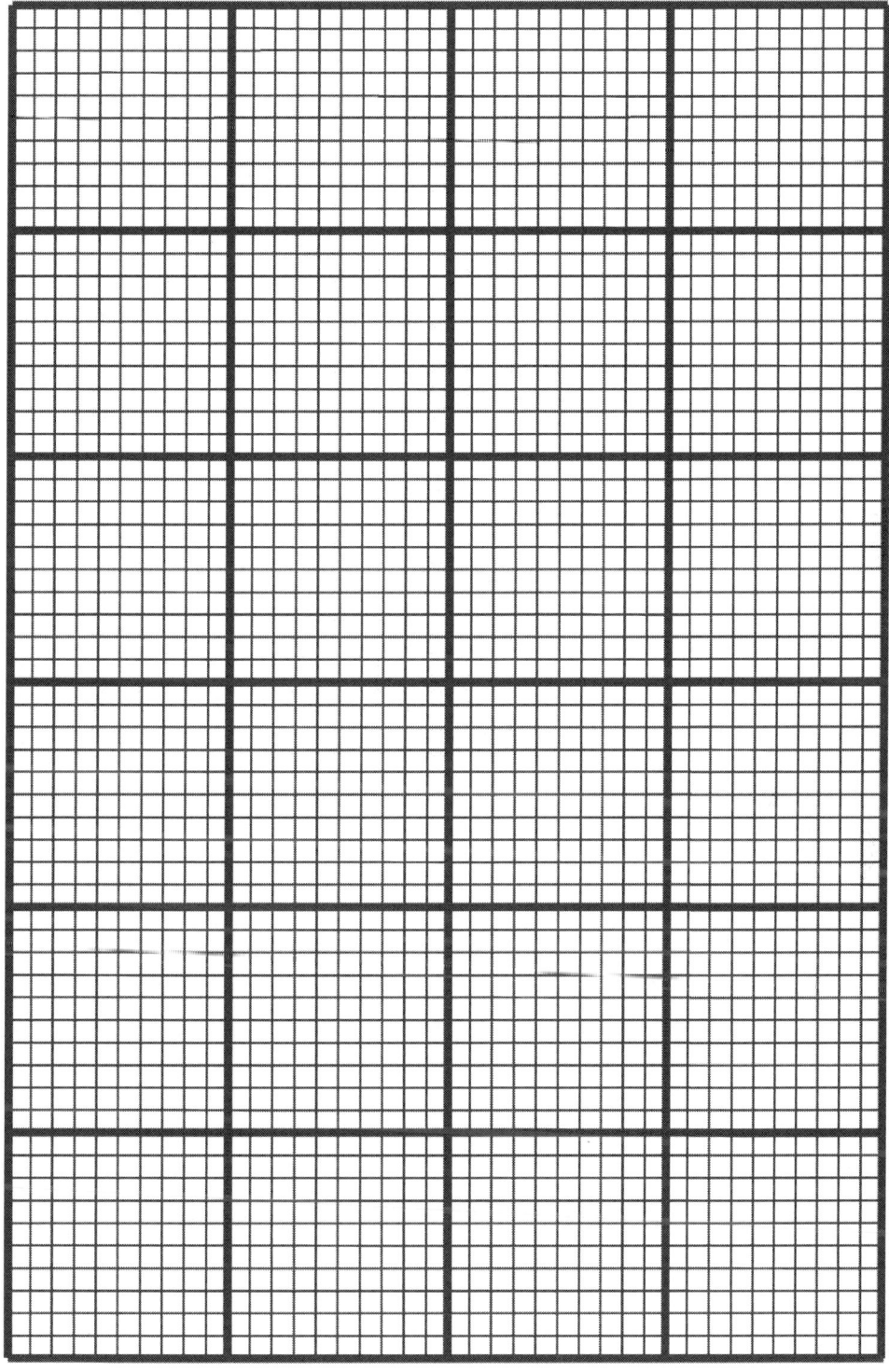

Floss Chart

	STRAND	TYPE	NUMBER	COLOR	ALTERNATE
•					
○					
■					
✚					
△					
◆					
=					
✖					
★					
⊙					
▫					
#					
▼					
☐					
☐					
▽					
→					
☽					

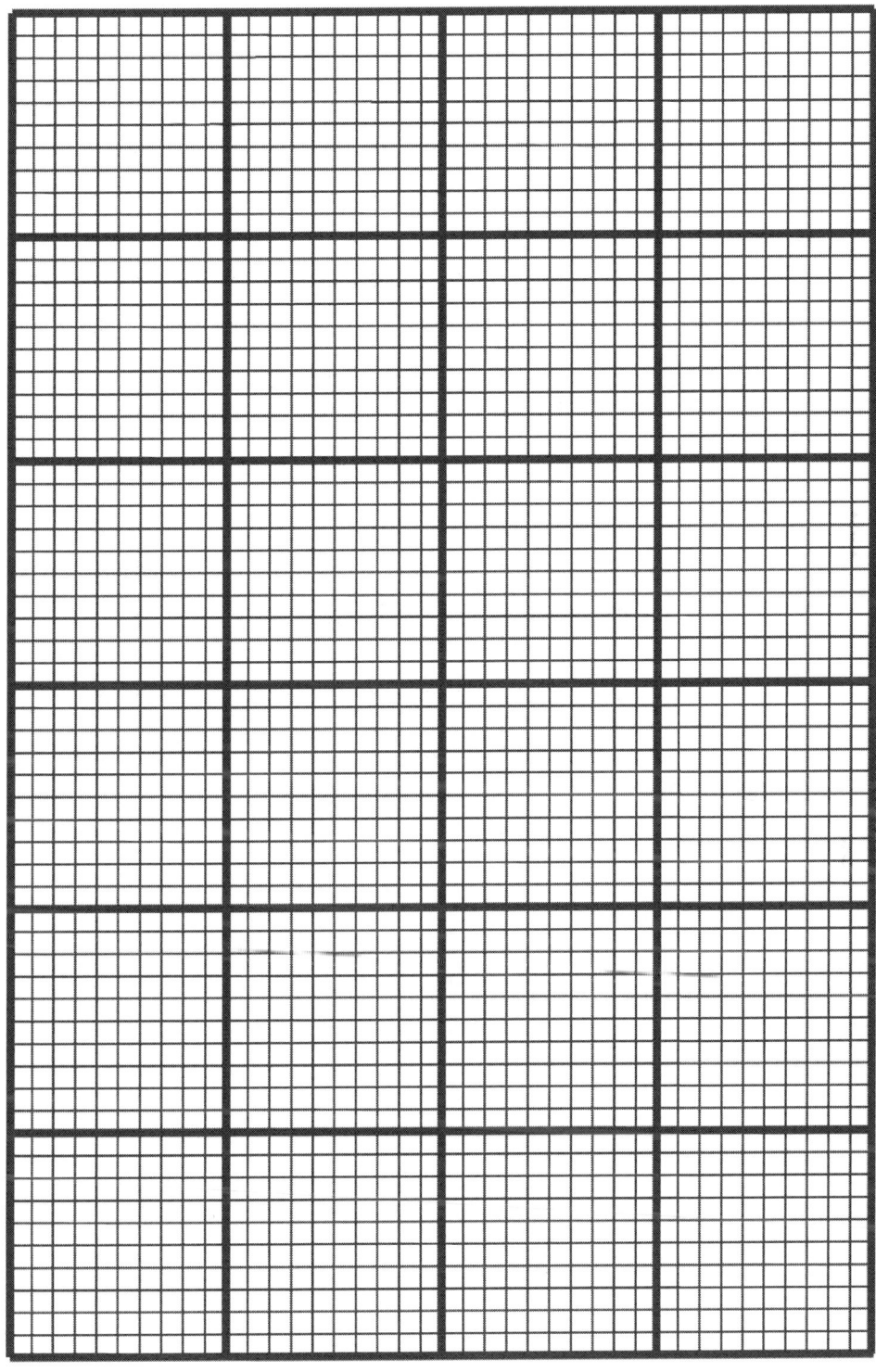

Floss Chart

	STRAND	TYPE	NUMBER	COLOR	ALTERNATE
•					
○					
■					
✚					
△					
◆					
=					
✖					
★					
⊙					
▣					
#					
▼					
☐					
☐					
▽					
→					
☽					

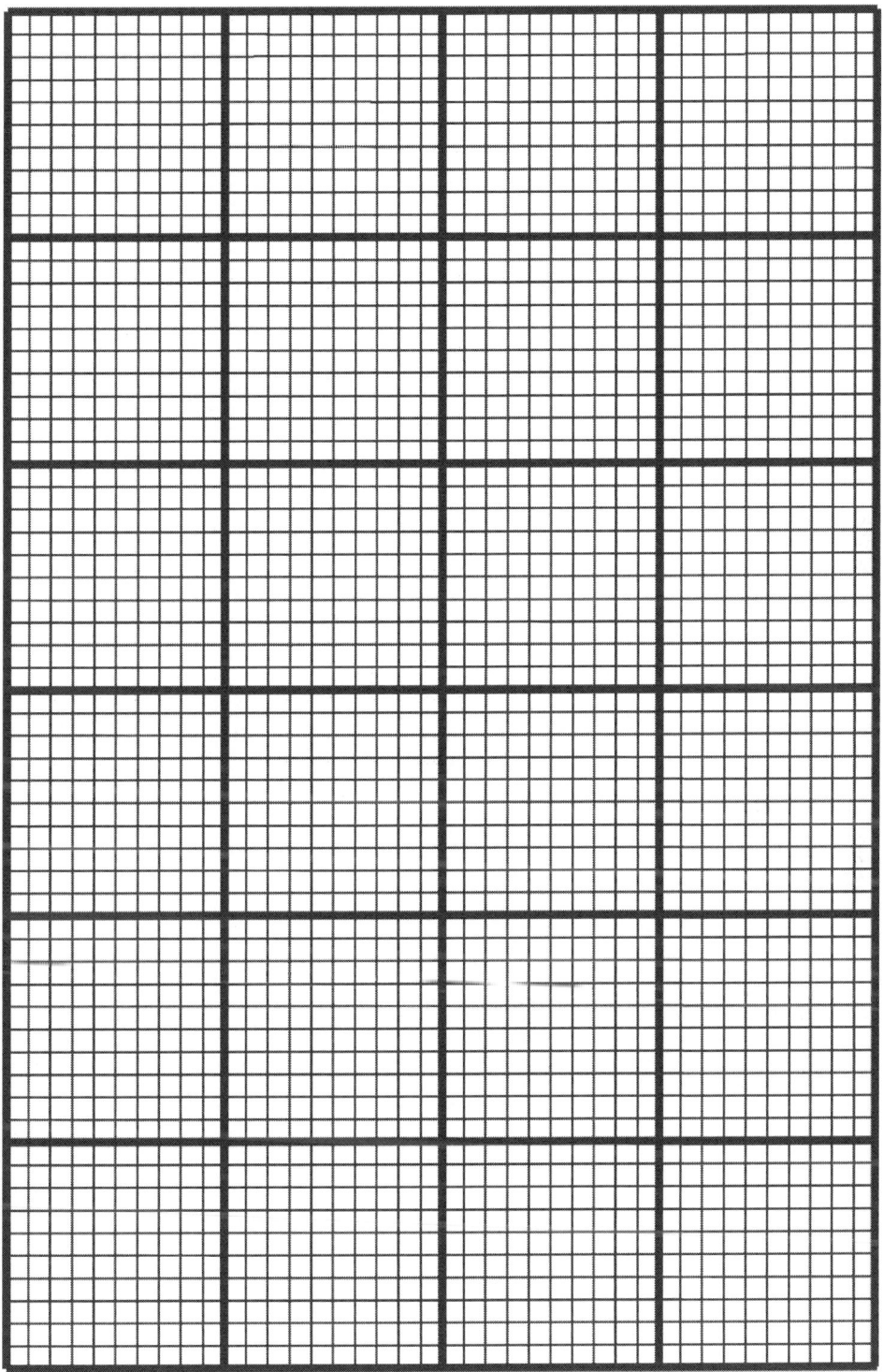

Floss Chart

	STRAND	TYPE	NUMBER	COLOR	ALTERNATE
•					
○					
■					
✚					
△					
◆					
=					
✖					
★					
⊙					
◻					
#					
▼					
☐					
☐					
▽					
→					
☽					

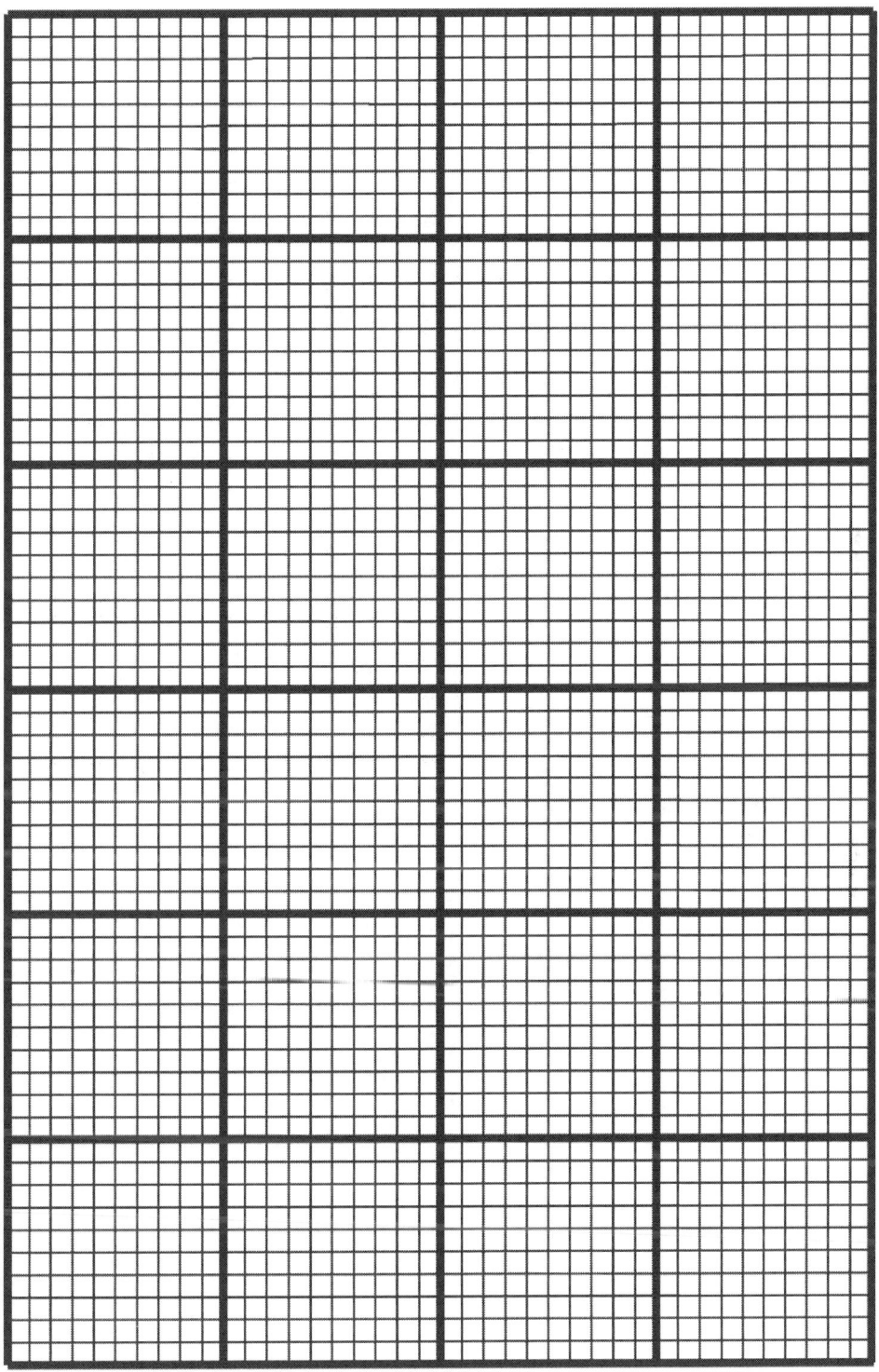

ABOUT HOOP & THREAD NEEDLEWORK DESIGN

Sisters, Arisa Williams and Kim O'Malley
design useful writing journals, diaries, doodle books,
sketch books, list creators and log books for you.
We wish you all the best things in life!

✕ ✕ ✕

Hoop & Thread Needlework Design – Fan-Craft-Tastic Fiber Art Makers Series
Cross Stitch & Needlepoint Chart and Pattern Sketchbook:
Four Sizes of Stitch Count Graphs on 10 Square Grid with Fill In Floss Charts

Brainstorm Journals - Love Me, Myself and I Series
Love Letters to Me: A Self Love Blank Lined Journal
1001 Reasons to Love Me: Create Your Own List

List Maker Maniac – I Heart Romance Series
1001 Reasons to Love Me: Fill In the Blank Personalized Book

Manufactured by Amazon.ca
Bolton, ON